Bloom's Modern Critical Interpretations

Bloom's Modern Critical Interpretations

John Steinbeck's
Short Stories

Edited and with an introduction by
Harold Bloom
Sterling Professor of the Humanities
Yale University

BLOOM'S
LITERARY CRITICISM
An Infobase Learning Company

Bloom's Modern Critical Interpretations: John Steinbeck's Short Stories

Copyright © 2011 by Infobase Learning
Introduction © 2011 by Harold Bloom

Bloom's Literary Criticism
An imprint of Infobase Learning
132 West 31st Street
New York NY 10001

Library of Congress Cataloging-in-Publication Data
John Steinbeck's short stories / edited and with an introduction by Harold Bloom.
    p. cm. — (Bloom's modern critical interpretations)
    Includes bibliographical references and index.
    ISBN 978-1-60413-271-7 (hardcover)
    1. Steinbeck, John, 1902–1968—Criticism and interpretation.   I. Bloom, Harold.
    PS3537.T3234Z71569 2011
    813'.52—dc22
                                                    2010052557

Bloom's Literary Criticism books are available at special discounts when purchased in bulk quantities for businesses, associations, institutions, or sales promotions. Please call our Special Sales Department in New York at (212)967-8800 or (800)322-8755.

You can find Bloom's Literary Criticism on the World Wide Web at
http://www.infobaselearning.com

Contributing editor: Pamela Loos
Cover design by Takeshi Takahashi
Composition by IBT Global, Troy NY
Cover printed by Yurchak Printing, Landisville, Pa.
Book printed and bound by Yurchak Printing, Landisville, Pa.
Date printed: April 2011
Printed in the United States of America

10 9 8 7 6 5 4 3 2 1

This book is printed on acid-free paper.

All links and Web addresses were checked and verified to be correct at the time of publication. Because of the dynamic nature of the Web, some addresses and links may have changed since publication and may no longer be valid.

Contents

Editor's Note

My introduction doubts the permanence of the liberal and humane Steinbeck, his better stories, such as "The Chrysanthemums," not leaving the indelible mark they should. While Richard F. Peterson acknowledges Steinbeck's debt to Lawrence, the former received some of the influence but none of the anxiety, which led to stagnation in his writing. Louis Owens then sketches the hero's quest as it unfolds throughout *The Red Pony*.

John H. Timmerman concedes to *The Red Pony*'s simplicity of tone and point of view while praising the collection's forceful grappling with death. Robert M. Benton turns his attention to "Flight," another example of simplicity coming at the expense of detail, complexity, and plausible motivation.

Susan Shillinglaw compares "The Chrysanthemums" to *Pygmalion*, after which Christopher S. Busch notes parallels between the story and "The White Quail."

John Ditsky examines the portrayal of women in *The Long Valley*, after which Mimi Reisel Gladstein explores affinities between Steinbeck and Faulkner in the early stories.

Stephen K. George returns to the women question, this time inevitably bringing Hemingway into the discussion. Charlotte Cook Hadella concludes the volume on a similar impulse, juxtaposing "The White Quail" with Welty's "A Curtain of Green."

HAROLD BLOOM

Introduction

It would be good to be able to say that the liberal and humane Steinbeck achieved permanence as a fiction writer. Alas, rereading the best of his novels and stories is a very mixed experience. *The Grapes of Wrath* is a period piece and, inevitably, will follow the path of all popular fiction and will be read only by social antiquarians.

An ambitious writer asks to be judged alongside the strongest of his contemporaries. Try to read William Faulkner's *As I Lay Dying* in conjunction with *The Grapes of Wrath*. Steinbeck is obliterated, as he is by Willa Cather and Theodore Dreiser, Ernest Hemingway and Scott Fitzgerald, Nathanael West and Flannery O'Connor. This saddens me, because I *want* Steinbeck to have been a great writer on the left. We lack such a figure, though Hemingway attempted to fill the lack in *For Whom the Bell Tolls* and failed. And yet even his failures remain more readable than Steinbeck's popular successes.

The late Anthony Burgess, a wise critic and undervalued novelist, remarked that Hemingway was Steinbeck's trouble. Take "Oklahoma" out of the first sentence of *The Grapes of Wrath* and substitute "the Basque lands," and you could drop the book's first two paragraphs into several contexts in *The Sun Also Rises*. What Steinbeck thought to be his own quasibiblical style is Hemingway all the way. What Steinbeck thought were his own portraits of enduring but frustrated women were D.H. Lawrence's. Compare Elisa Allen in "The Chrysanthemums," one of Steinbeck's better short stories, to March in Lawrence's "The Fox." Influence without anxiety produces stagnation; a touch of the anxiety of influence might have benefited Steinbeck.

There are other difficulties in trying to reread Steinbeck with any rigor. The Okies of *The Grapes of Wrath* never were: Steinbeck knew Oklahoma

1

about as well as he knew Afghanistan. That might not matter, except that Steinbeck's poor whites are contemporary with Faulkner's, and the Joads as a literary creation lack the aesthetic dignity and persuasive substantiality of the Bundrens in *As I Lay Dying*. Floyd Watkins, a quarter century ago, demonstrated this as well as the shadow quality of the Joads compared to the rural poor of Eudora Welty and Robert Penn Warren.

You can argue, if you wish, that Steinbeck's Okies are a visionary creation, but then you are likely to find them dwarfed by their cinematic representations in John Ford's *The Grapes of Wrath*, as superior to Steinbeck's novel as Herman Melville's *Moby-Dick* is in comparison to John Huston's filmed travesty of it.

Aesthetic defense of *The Grapes of Wrath* is perhaps still barely possible, but to get through *In Dubious Battle* now is a dreadful struggle. Steinbeck remains a popular writer, but so is the hopelessly, implacably doctrinaire Ayn Rand, dear to many rightwing readers. There are depths beneath depths in popular fiction: What should one make of John Grisham? I cannot force my way through more than a few pages. It is a sorrow that Steinbeck, a "worthy" writer, as Burgess said, should have fallen into the cosmos of period pieces.

RICHARD F. PETERSON

The God in the Darkness:
A Study of John Steinbeck and D. H. Lawrence

When John Steinbeck expressed his admiration for D. H. Lawrence, he was acknowledging a writer who had an intense effect upon him for a brief period of time.[1] Lawrence's general influence on Steinbeck was not so pervasive that Steinbeck's writing continually reflects Lawrencean themes or that the careers of the two men coincide in terms of the development of their fiction. Instead, as Peter Lisca points out, in *To A God Unknown* and in many of the stories in *The Long Valley*, Steinbeck seems preoccupied with psychological interests that reflect a possible reading of D. H. Lawrence.[2] It is only within this brief but critical period of time during Steinbeck's development as a writer that Lawrence's fiction provided a model for Steinbeck; and, even though Steinbeck's reading of Lawrence greatly influenced the ritual as well as the psychological nature of the works of this period, the study of the Lawrence-Steinbeck relationship needs to be further qualified by the apparent limited amount of Lawrence's fiction actually read by Steinbeck.

Lisca does not pursue the implications of his statement on Lawrence and Steinbeck, but he does immediately follow his statement on Steinbeck's psychological interests by noting that "Elisa Allen in 'The Chrysanthemums,' Mary Teller in 'The White Quail,' Amy Hawkins in 'Johnny Bear,' and the anonymous woman in 'The Snake' are psychological portraits of frustrated

From *Steinbeck's Literary Dimension: A Guide to Comparative Studies*, edited by Tetsumaro Hayashi, pp. 67–82. Copyright © 1972 by Tetsumaro Hayashi.

females."[3] Even though Lisca's juxtaposition provides little information for the task of determining the extent of Lawrence's influence on *To A God Unknown* and its great emphasis on male activity, it does provide an area of consideration that, when united with other Lawrencean themes more directly concerned with *To A God Unknown*, narrows the search for specific works of Lawrence read by Steinbeck to a definite period of development in Lawrence's career.

The idea of the frustrated female initially establishes a general connection between several of the stories in *The Long Valley* and the fiction of Lawrence that extends back to Lettie in *The White Peacock* and encompasses most of Lawrence's major works. This sense of female frustration, particularly for Lawrence, is sexual and it is usually manifested by the female through a denial of her own sexuality and her conscious attempt to possess the male by undermining his natural position of authority in the male-female relationship. In Steinbeck's "The White Quail" Mary Teller's willful denial of the real world and her acceptance of the artificial world of her trim and ordered garden in its place reveals her own lack of female vitality, but the effect that her obsession with the garden has on her husband, Harry, is to deny his manhood, indirectly revealed in her contempt for his business practices, so that her girlhood dream can be realized and preserved. She retains her innocence (spirit) but, at the same time, isolates and devitalizes Harry's maleness. She functions, in relation to the male, in somewhat the same fashion as Mrs. Morel, in *Sons and Lovers*, who usurps the male role of authority in the family and, in the process, denies the maleness in her husband and prevents her sons from having fulfilling relationships with women other than herself. Despite the symbolic impact of Harry's killing of the white quail, his sense of complete loneliness and desolation at the end of the story marks his fate as similar to that of Anton Skrebensky in *The Rainbow* and Gerald Crich in *Women in Love*, two men victimized by the female who withholds her essential self from the male and, at the same time, sucks away his male vitality.

Though the Lawrencean woman who insists on denying her natural female role of submission usually responds destructively towards her male partner, Lawrence did not completely fault the female figure in the breakdown of the male-female relationship. He believed that the woman assumed the unnatural position of dominance because modern man had lost the sexual potency to keep her in a submissive role. Anton Skrebensky is destroyed as a male by Ursula Erangwen's withdrawal from him, but her rejection of the man is necessitated by his failure to respond completely to Ursula's need to be fulfilled as natural woman (universal being) rather than Ursula (personal being). In other words, Ursula wants to lose her identity with the world, all the "old dead things," and be restored to her natural place in the cosmos.

Rather than seeing himself as the center of the universe and the female as a vital yet subordinate part of the cosmos, this type of Lawrence male has a love for dead and mechanical things that immobilizes him to the extent that, as he builds his world, he fails to realize his own male uniqueness; and, to fill the void created, he turns back to the female for comfort, security, and even his identity.[4]

The failure of the male to define himself in natural relationship with the female and to provide the source of power for the female figures is treated prominently in the stories in *The Long Valley* which deal directly with the plight of the male. In "The Harness" Peter Randall's trapped condition extends beyond the grave, as his dead wife retains her domination of his life. Jim Moore, in "The Murder," must learn to reach the deep passionate nature of his wife or accept the prospect of repeated instances of cuckoldry. The final condition for the male who refuses to assert his natural male authority is isolation and loneliness. Jim's act of violence is the proper response to the dark side of his wife, and it restores him to his natural position as dominant male. Harry Teller can destroy the symbol of his wife's spirituality, but in the real world his condition remains the same: "'What a dirty skunk, to kill a thing she loves so much.' He dropped his head and looked at the floor. 'I'm lonely,' he said. 'Oh, Lord, I'm so lonely!'"[5]

The despair that comes from the deterioration of the male-female relationship is most revealingly presented in the condition of one of the frustrated females of *The Long Valley*. Eliza Allen, of "The Chrysanthemums," is a woman of great vitality, but her sense of being alive, of being in vital contact with nature, is not confirmed by the male world. Her husband, Henry, does not function importantly in the major encounter of the story, but Steinbeck reveals Henry's insensitivity to the female through his male activities and his conversation with Eliza. Henry sees the world through male eyes and, in turn, recognizes only the male's capacity for passion; he is shocked by Eliza's interest in prize fights, and, when previously faced with the physical presence of an aroused rather than usually placid wife, he responds by telling her that she looks "so nice."

Eliza's attraction to the wandering tinker is a manifestation of her desire for the freedom of the male, but, at the same time, her fascination for his way of life is evoked by images that suggest it is her female sexuality that needs to be set free:

'I've never lived as you do, but I know what you mean. When the night is dark—why, the stars are sharp-pointed, and there's quiet. Why, you rise up and up! Every pointed star gets driven into your body. It's like that. Hot and sharp and—lovely.' [p. 18]

When she finds her gift, the chrysanthemums, lying along the road, she recognizes again the treachery of the male, the willingness of the male to exploit her naturalness for profit or comfort. Her interest in the prize fights, like her desire for the wine, is a desperate attempt to retain the passion aroused by her encounter with the tinker. When her husband suggests that she will not enjoy the fights, she accepts the wine as a substitute; but her sense of female defeat and her loss of sexual potency is overpowering: "She turned up her coat collar so he could not see that she was crying weakly—like an old woman" (p. 23).

The period of Lawrence's most violent reaction to the deterioration of the male-female relationship, what H. M. Daleski terms as Lawrence's "One Up, One Down" period, is particularly relevant to the relationship between Lawrence and Steinbeck. What distinguishes this period from others in which Lawrence was also concerned with this basic relationship is the development of a leadership theme. At this time, Lawrence also emphasized characters who, according to Daleski,

> are to be concerned with 'advance and increase,' that they are to be 'projected into a region of greater abstraction,' of 'pure thought and abstracted instrumentality,' in their journey 'into the unknown'; in terms of Lawrence's attribution of male and female qualities, that is to say, they are to be engaged in characteristic male activity.[6]

This period of male dominance in Lawrence's fiction invites a comparison between the new hero of Lawrence and Steinbeck's natural leader, Joseph Wayne, of *To A God Unknown*. The novels written by Lawrence during this period develop the idea of a natural leader, who maintains power through his intimate contact with the cosmos and his ability to translate that concept into a myth that revitalizes the souls of the people. Lawrence begins, in *Aaron's Rod* with the dilemma of Aaron Sissoa, who through the guidance of his friend, Rawdon Lilly, discovers the necessity for the reestablishment of male friendship and male activity in the world as a means to nurture the male sexual potency back to a condition of health and power. In *Kangaroo* and *The Plumed Serpent*, Aaron's discovery is transmitted into male action. The relationship between Richard Somers, the Lawrence figure in *Kangaroo*, and Ben Cooley or Kangaroo, the leader of the Diggers, a secret military organization, is a study of the potential for the assertion of male power in the world of politics. When Somers rejects Kangaroo and his world of political activity, he does so on the grounds that Kangaroo's form of male activity is restricted to the workings of the mind or spirit. It forces the lower self to respond to the dictates of the mind-will and, in the process, destroys the vital, passionate part of man. Somers' response to the dying Kangaroo anticipates *The Plumed Serpent* and sounds the note of comparison between Don Ramon of *The Plumed Serpent* and Steinbeck's Joseph Wayne:

> The only thing one can stick to is one's own isolated being, and the God in whom it is rooted. And the only thing to look to is the God who fulfills one from the dark. And the only thing to wait for is for men to find their aloneness and their God in the darkness.[7]

Both Don Ramon and Joseph Wayne are actualizations of the heroic male described by Richard Somers. Both characters find their "aloneness," which is their sense of individual contact with the surrounding universe; and both find the "God in the darkness" which is the rediscovery of their intimate connection with the mystery of the cosmos. Don Ramon expresses this idea of the God-man through his attempt to revitalize the old Mexican God, Quetzalcoatl. The importance of this god figure for Don Ramon is that he represents the entire span of life; he is "lord of both ways." Don Ramon rejects Christianity as a natural religion for man because it appeals strictly to the spirit and must be understood consciously to have an effect. What man needs is not a god of the mind, but rather a god who encompasses spirit and soul, both the above and the below. In Quetzalcoatl, the Plumed Serpent, Don Ramon has found a symbol of heaven (Quetzal-bird) and earth (Coatl-serpent).

Don Ramon's part in restoring Quetzalcoatl to man is that of First Man of Quetzalcoatl. In this role, Don Ramon becomes one of the Initiators of the Earth. He further describes himself as one of the natural aristocrats of the world, a man who is defined and prevented from merging with other aristocrats by his race, but, nevertheless, a man who is set apart from the common mass of his race by his intense awareness of complete physical being. He wants Mexicans to learn the name, language, and rituals of Quetzalcoatl so that they may also speak in their own blood consciousness. The revival of the old gods of Mexico by their new prophet, however, is a more conscious attempt to apprehend and bring into harmony the basic duality of existence. This abstract event is most completely actualized in the marriage of Kate and Cipriano performed to the primitive rhythm of ancient ceremony, consummated by the coming of the rain, the perfect expression in nature of the unity of above and below.

Steinbeck's Joseph Wayne has the potential to be a priest of the people. After his last meeting with Joseph, Father Angelo is shaken by "the force of the man." His thoughts capture the "threat" to the church posed by Joseph and, at the same time, offer a striking parallel between the natures of Don

Ramon and Joseph Wayne: "'Thank God this man has no message. Thank God he has no will to be remembered, to be believed in.' And in sudden heresy, 'else there might be a new Christ here in the West.'"[8] Joseph, like Don Ramon, is a member of the natural aristocracy of man. He possesses the same phallic power of a Don Ramon, and he, too, feels confirmed in that power by his sense of being one with the universe (his desire for the land) and his acceptance of the heritage of the race (the traditional blessing from his father). Once Joseph arrives at Nuestra Señora, the long valley of our lady, he becomes aware of the coming together of his biological and racial heritage, "for his father and the new land were one" (p. 5). Though Joseph's god is unknown, the power that he senses in the universe becomes polarized in the figure of the father. He consigns his father's spirit to a giant oak tree; thus, again, he unites spirit and nature in the same way that Don Ramon does through the image of Quetzalcoatl. What remains for Joseph is to summon his brothers to settle in the valley, and for Joseph, himself, to enter into the rhythm of life by marrying and giving his seed to a woman capable of receiving it.

In both *The Plumed Serpent* and *To A God Unknown*, the power of the god is distilled in the man. As Rama, wife of Joseph's brother, Thomas, explains,

> 'I tell you this man is not a man, unless he is all men. The strength, the resistance, the long and stumbling thinking of all men, and all the joy and suffering, too, cancelling each other out and yet remaining in the contents. He is all these, a repository for a little piece of each man's soul, and more than that, a symbol of the earth's soul.' [p. 66]

If Don Ramon becomes sometimes too formal and even dull, it is because he is attempting to articulate a godliness that has its source in the blood consciousness of man. He faces the task of formulating a Lawrencean philosophical position in the language of a primitive religion and people. Yet he remains in complete control of his own sense of being and preserves that sense of aloneness and detachment Lawrence believes would lead to the "God in the darkness."

Joseph Wayne's sense of power is more closely aligned with his unconscious urges, since he rarely attempts to articulate his primitive awareness of the God-in-the-man.[9] Because of this, his natural religion, his tree and rock worship, seems more a part of the man than Don Ramon's religion of Quetzalcoatl. The situation Joseph Wayne encounters also eventually becomes entirely different from that faced by Don Ramon. Once Joseph's brother, Burton, girdles his father's tree, Joseph is faced with a crisis of the land rather than of the people. When the following winter comes, it brings no rain with it. The baptismal act of nature that announces the rebirth, growth, and unity of all living things is now denied Joseph Wayne and the land. His role of King-god, the god-like man who dominates and breathes his life into the land, is drastically changed. He now becomes the Fisher King and must bear a new responsibility for the now dying land. According to Joseph Fontenrose, "Joseph is a Frazerian divine king who must die because he has lost his divine potency."[10] Joseph's shift from King-god to Fisher King marks an important distinction between the heroes of *To A God Unknown* and *The Plumed Serpent*. It also suggests the likelihood that, despite the basic similarities between the two characters in their awareness of their complete physical being and their intimate connection with the cosmos, Steinbeck may not have borrowed directly from *The Plumed Serpent*. A more probable source of influence, one that offers the possibility of sacrifice as a means for restoring the natural order of things but still supports the concept of the natural, heroic man presented by Lawrence in *The Plumed Serpent*, is a collection of short stories entitled, *The Woman Who Rode Away*.[11] Three stories in the collection, "Sun," "The Woman Who Rode Away," and "The Man Who Loved Islands," seem particularly related to the completion of Steinbeck's *To A God Unknown*. Added to this possibility of a direct influence, moreover, is the further possibility that several stories in the Lawrence collection which are studies of frustrated, sexless females may have influenced the creation of those equally frustrated females who appear in those stories in *The Long Valley* previously mentioned.

Even though the main characters of "Sun" and "The Woman Who Rode Away" are females, the stories are comparative with *To A God Unknown* in imagery and theme. "Sun" is the story of Juliet, a bored and tired American woman who is brought back into intimate connection with the natural world through her worship of the powers of the sun. As she lies naked on a rocky bluff of a Mediterranean island and absorbs the rays of the sun, she is restored to a new and vital sense of femaleness. Though the story is united thematically with *To A God Unknown* in its stress on the close relationship between man and the cosmos, what is of particular importance for the Lawrence-Steinbeck relationship is the similarity between the phallic scenery of "Sun" and that of *To A God Unknown*. In both works, the power of nature to penetrate the human soul is presented in sexual terms. When Juliet bathes naked in the sun, she can feel it penetrate her body. The sun pulsates its warmth "even into her bones, even into her emotions and thoughts."[12] At the place where she bathes she notices "one cypress tree, with a pallid, thick trunk, and a tip that leaned over, flexible, up in the blue. It stood like a guardian looking to sea; or a low, silvery candle whose huge flame was darkness against light: earth sending up her proud tongue of gloom" (p. 25). The idea of Juliet coming under the power of *phallos* is even further suggested by a fertility ritual in which she wanders naked in the gully between the two estates and encounters the vital, dark-faced peasant whose passion and seed she desires but cannot have because of her husband's return from the mechanical and hostile world she now dreads.

Similarly, Joseph Wayne's feelings for the land are closely related to sexual urgings. He senses a "curious femaleness" about the land, and when his possessiveness of the land becomes a passion he responds in a way that inverts the passive acceptance of Juliet:

> He stamped his feet into the soft earth. Then the exultance grew to be a sharp pain of desire that ran through his body in a hot river. He flung himself face downward on the grass and pressed his cheek against the wet stems. His fingers gripped the wet grass and tore it out, and gripped again. His thighs beat heavily on the earth. [p. 8]

After his violent embrace, Joseph is left tired and frightened by his "moment of passion," but, as he rests that evening, the act is presented again to him in phallic scenery similar to that viewed by Juliet as she lies naked in the sun:

> After a while the honey-colored moon arose behind the eastern ridge. Before it was clear of the hills, the golden face looked through bars of pine-trunks. Then for a moment a black sharp pine tree pierced the moon and was withdrawn as the moon arose. [p. 8]

Even Juliet's passage along the gully and its suggestiveness of a fertility rite is similarly evoked in Joseph's entry through the pass with his bride, Elizabeth. According to Joseph Fontenrose, the event is

> fertility ritual and a *rite de passage*, complete with scapegoat sacrifice. For Benjamin was killed at this time while engaged in the sex act, representing the mock king who was killed to insure the safety of the real king; and the killer was not punished but vanished for a time like the killers of the sacred ox in Athens.[13]

"The Woman Who Rode Away" and "The Man Who Loved Islands" have a more thematic relationship with *To A God Unknown*. If the two Lawrence stories are examined together, they present a study of the scapegoat king whose death is required for the refertilization of the land. "The Man Who Loved Islands" tells about a man who isolates himself from humanity by moving from island to smaller island until he is left alone at the mercy of the destructive elements. The similarity between this Lawrencean hero and Joseph Wayne exists in the attitude of the people toward their acknowledged leader and the way in which each man negates the possibility of human contact as he becomes increasingly obsessed with a barren, dying world. The hero of Lawrence's story is called "the Master" by those who are initially allowed to share the island as his servants. One of the women, the farm-wife, also recognizes qualities in him that "made you think of Our Saviour Himself" (p. 207). Similarly, when Elizabeth, at her wedding, tries to imagine the figure of Christ, she creates "the face, the youthful beard, the piercing puzzled eyes of Joseph, who stood beside her" (p. 47). On other occasions, both Father Angelo and Juanito recognize the Christ in Joseph, but whereas Father Angelo sees the power of Christ in the man, Juanito recognizes the defeated, crucified Christ.

The difference between "the Master" and Joseph Wayne lies in the nature and significance of their deaths. Lawrence's hero is driven into isolation more by his dread of intimate human contact and his fear of betrayal than by his need to restore his natural relationship with the cosmos. His destruction during the snow and cold of winter parallels the mindless death of Gerald Crich in *Women in Love*. His death, unlike that of Joseph Wayne, offers no hope for the restoration of life. As he dies he imagines himself in the midst of summer; but the illusion quickly fades and he becomes aware again of the approaching snow. Joseph Wayne's eventual isolation is more of an indication of his own need to accept total responsibility for the dying land. Any sacrifice, human or animal, proves irrelevant as the universe seems to await the death of the King-god himself. Accordingly, as the life flows out of the veins of Joseph's slashed wrists, he becomes aware of the growing darkness and the approaching rain. The moment, however, is not illusory; as Joseph dies "the storm thickened, and covered the world with darkness, and with the rush of waters" (p. 179).

The idea of human sacrifice as the means of restoring the harmony between man and the land is explored by Lawrence in "The Woman Who Rode Away." In this story, one of Lawrence's bored American women goes on a quest to find a mysterious tribe descended from the Aztecs. When she wanders upon the tribe they take her, almost with her consent, as a human sacrifice. What is important in this story beyond the depiction of the death-will of the white woman is the reason the Indians want the woman as a blood sacrifice. They feel her voluntary coming is a sign that their mystic contact with the cosmos, denied them by the domination of the land by the whites, is to be restored. In other words, her death will herald the reestablishment of the living connection between their people and the land.

The general relationship between "The Woman Who Rode Away" and *To A God Unknown* is the Fisher King theme. This similarity, by itself, raises no serious question of influence since the writings of J. G. Frazer and Jessie Weston were familiar to both writers. Yet when the similarity is added to those between "Sun," "The Man Who Loved Islands" and *To A God Unknown*, the evidence of possible influence increases. Of particular importance in directly comparing "The Woman Who Rode Away" and *To A God Unknown* are the presentations of the death scenes of the major characters. Lawrence's "girl from Berkeley" is carried on a litter through a valley covered with snow. The bearers enter a group of pinetrees and follow the stream bed of a now dry stream until they come to a wall of solid rock. Behind a huge, inverted pinnacle of ice, naked priests are waiting in a cave for her arrival. The woman is stripped of her native garments and taken into the cave for the blood sacrifice. She is laid on a large flat stone as the priests with their knives wait for the death moment, which will come when the sun completely fills the cave.

Though Joseph Wayne takes his own life (the woman in Lawrence's story never resists her fate), several similarities are apparent in the cause of the deaths of the two characters. Joseph sacrifices himself for the same reason that the Indians take the white woman's life. Just as the Indian priests await the sun as the signal to slay their victim and reassert their natural heritage of the sun and the moon, Joseph slashes his wrists to avow his oneness with the land. As blood gushes from his wrists the elements respond accordingly. As Joseph loses consciousness of his body, the needed rain begins to fall. Almost at the moment of death, Joseph articulates the connection between man and the cosmos sought through the blood sacrifice: "'I am the land,' he said 'and I am the rain. The grass will grow out of me in a little while'" (p. 26).

The sacrificial settings are also similar in the two works. The rock or mountain, as the heart of the land, functions as the place of sacrifice; and, in each story, the rock-mountain contains a cave and provides the source for a now dried-up stream. It is also completely surrounded by pine trees. In each setting, the cave is central to the significance of the death of the main character. In "The Woman Who Rode Away" the cave becomes the place of execution, but, because of the intent of the act, it actually becomes the place where the redemption of the people begins. Joseph Wayne dies while lying atop the rock, yet as the blood flows from his wrists onto the rock, it becomes obvious that he now provides the life stream that previously flowed from the cave. From out of the cave previously came the life flow, the hope for man; but that flow has now become the blood of man and woman. The cave now seems to symbolize the darkness in the human soul which contains the God in man, for it is man's own blood that restores him to his proper place in the mystery of the cosmos.

Certain stories in *The Woman Who Rode Away* which directly approach the problem of the male-female relationship offer further parallels between Lawrence and Steinbeck and increase the likelihood of an influence.[14] Domineering females and their dominated or defiant male partners frequently provide the subject matter for stories in both *The Woman Who Rode Away* and *The Long Valley*. Of the frustrated, sexless females who appear in the Lawrence stories, those in "Two Blue Birds" and "None of That" are particularly similar to the Steinbeck women in "The White Quail" and "The Snake." "Two Blue Birds" is Lawrence's rather lightly satirical treatment of a sexless love triangle between two females and a male. The struggle for control over the male is waged between his wife and his secretary. The wife attempts to conquer her rival by forcing her will in opposition to the husband and the secretary, while the secretary prefers to gain control over the male by assuming the passive role of complete obedience. Of particular importance in comparing "Two Blue Birds" with "The White Quail" is Lawrence's use of bird imagery to define the character of the female. Lawrence accentuates the lack of sexual vitality in the struggle of the two females by presenting the parallel skirmish of two blue birds. The similarity between the ineffectual fight between the blue birds and the insignificant clash of words between the two females is brought home rather forcibly when the two human combatants face each other while dressed in blue.

In "The White Quail" Mary Teller's lack of sexual vitality is revealed by Mary herself, when she identifies with the rare white quail which drinks at the pool in her garden. Her appeal to her husband, Harry, to kill the prowling cat further indicates her fear of any physical contact with the world outside her garden. She denies the world outside the jurisdiction of her will. Harry's dilemma is that he, too, is dominated by the female. His decision to kill the quail rather than the cat symbolizes a brief assertion of his maleness, but, at the end of the story, his fate remains that of the sexually vigorous male who, because of the female's dominance, acknowledges and accepts the conditions of isolation and despair.

Ethel Cane in "None of That" and the mysterious woman in "The Snake" are two other females unwilling to participate physically in a male world. They are comparative on a much more ominous basis than Mary Teller and Lawrence's "two blue birds." The woman in "The Snake" gratifies vicariously her obsession to dominate and identify with the male; she watches her newly acquired possession, a male rattlesnake, methodically kill and devour a laboratory rat. During the experience the woman identifies with the snake, the victimizer. She desires the male role denied to her by her own nature. She cannot participate in her natural role with the male, so she is forced to own and admire the male power she cannot cope with as a woman.

Ethel Cane, of "None of That," also refuses the female role; she wants "none of *that*" physical contact with the male. Her admiration for Cuestra, the matador, parallels the fascination of Steinbeck's strange female for the rattlesnake. Ethel also has a fantastic desire to possess, to assert her female will and power upon the male world. She claims, moreover, that her desire is for the world of imagination not the physical male world. In Cuestra's performance in the bullring she witnesses brutalized life idealized into an art form. Just as Steinbeck's woman identifies with the ritual of the snake's performance, Ethel responds to the quick, cruel movements of the matador, her "beast with an imagination." Yet what she really admires in Cuestra's performance is a deadliness that counteracts Hemingway's aesthetics of the bullring, and instead brings the fictional worlds of Lawrence and Steinbeck together again in theme and imagery. When Ethel says that she sees a "marvelous thing" in Cuestra, her male companion and escort replies "But so has a rattlesnake a marvelous thing in him: two things, one in his mouth one in his tail. But I didn't want to get a response out of a rattlesnake" (p. 299). Dr. Phillips, in "The Snake," makes the inverse comparison by suggesting that "it's better than a bullfight if you look at it one way, and it's simply a snake eating his dinner if you look at it another" (p. 80).

The conclusions of the two stories are presented differently. Ethel is raped by a bullfight gang after she is invited to Cuestra's house. Later, she commits suicide to preserve her imaginative vision of an idealized world. Steinbeck's snake lover simply disappears, and is never seen again by Dr. Phillips. Yet, though the events are not parallel, the effect of the endings is quite similar. In both cases, the female is presented as an unnatural being. Her end signifies her refusal or inability to exist or survive as a woman in the real world.

The sexually frustrated female and the male-god asserting his oneness with the mystery of the cosmos offer striking counterparts for the male-female relationship. For Lawrence, they represent individuals who are very much a part of a world that is based upon the interaction of the male and the female. The extremes they represent are indicative of the perpetual struggle of both sexes for dominance and the destructive potential in a war of wills. Appropriately, in Lawrence's final period of writing, exemplified by *Lady Chatterley's Lover*, there is again an appeal for reconciliation, for a way in which man and woman can preserve their separate identities but still engage in an intimate sexual and imaginative union.

The frustrated female, the King-god, is more unusual in Steinbeck's world. In much of Steinbeck's fiction after the period which includes *To A God Unknown* and *The Long Valley* the female often provides the source of strength for the faltering male. The male, on the other hand, is presented more and more as part of the group organism, a man no greater than the function he performs in relation to his social or political group. The period in which the fictional worlds of Lawrence and Steinbeck come together is brief, but the contact spawns some of the strongest and strangest characters in Steinbeck's fiction. More importantly, it allowed Steinbeck to pursue an important area of human feelings and responsiveness. His eventual movement away from a world so intensely personal in its psychological and sexual orientation to one more social and moral in content is less the artist's retreat as it is a recognition of the nature of his artistic sensibilities.

NOTES

1. Harry Thornton Moore, *The Novels of John Steinbeck* (Chicago: Normandie House, 1939), p. 92.

2. *The Wide World of John Steinbeck* (New Brunswick, New Jersey: Rutgers University Press, 1958), p. 95.

3. Ibid.

4. Gerald Crich of *Women in Love* and Sir Clifford Chatterley of *Lady Chatterley's Lover* are the most striking examples of the Lawrencean male who is unable to respond to the passionate side of life and is forced to seek the comfort of the maternal figure.

5. *The Long Valley* (New York: Viking Press, 1938), p. 42. All subsequent quotations will be taken from this edition.

6. *The Forked Flame: A Study of D. H. Lawrence* (Evanston, Illinois: Northwestern University Press, 1965), p. 189.

7. *Kangaroo* (New York: Viking Press, 1963), p. 335.

8. *To A God Unknown* (New York: Bantam Books, 1968), p. 172.

9. I refer you again to Father Angelo's comment on Joseph Wayne's potential power as a religious leader of the people.

10. *John Steinbeck: An Introduction and Interpretation* (New York: Holt, Rinehart, and Winston, 1963), p. 16.

11. I am indebted to Bobby L. Smith, a Lawrence scholar and admirer of Steinbeck, for suggesting *The Woman Who Rode Away* as the probable source of Lawrence's influence on Steinbeck. The stories were published in America in 1928.

12. *The Woman Who Rode Away* (New York: Alfred A. Knopf, 1930), p. 26.

13. Fontenrose, p. 16.

14. No story in *The Woman Who Rode Away* parallels the stories of youth in *The Long Valley*. There are, however, some similarities between Lawrence's "The Prussian Officer," a story appearing in an earlier collection, and "Flight." Both stories present in vivid and brutal terms the ordeal of escape and death for the young man who has committed murder. "The Vigilante," in its equation of the experience of the lynching mob and the sex act, also seems under the influence of Lawrence, but I have not been able to trace the story to a specific source. "The Leader of the People" is indebted more to Steinbeck's developing ideas on the group man than Lawrence's concept of the leader.

LOUIS OWENS

The Red Pony: *Commitment and Quest*

Like *To a God Unknown* and "Flight," the four stories that make up *The Red Pony* are set in the foothills of the Santa Lucia Mountains on the California coastline. And once again, in these stories dealing with Jody Tiflin's growing awareness of the mysteries of death, the western mountains stand out as symbols of both death and the unknown.

Of this book, Steinbeck stated:

> *The Red Pony* was written . . . when there was desolation in my family. The first death had occurred. And the family, which every child believes to be immortal, was shattered. Perhaps this is the first adulthood of any man or woman. The first tortured question of "why?" and the acceptance and the child becomes a man. *The Red Pony* was an attempt, an experiment if you wish, to set down this acceptance and growth.[38]

Critics have customarily accepted this reading of the stories in *The Red Pony*, finding, with a hint from Steinbeck, that the book is a kind of *Bildungsroman*, an initiation cycle in which Jody Tiflin becomes increasingly aware of what Arnold L. Goldsmith has termed "an organic theory of life ending in death which in turn produces life." Joseph Fontenrose suggests that Jody,

From *John Steinbeck's Re-Vision of America*, pp. 46–58. Copyright © 1985 by the University of Georgia Press.

17

through his exposure to increasing responsibilities, passes from childhood to adulthood. Fontenrose calls the book "a story of initiation comparable to Faulkner's 'The Bear.'" Goldsmith, in turn, equates Jody with Hemingway's Nick Adams growing toward manhood. While Peter Lisca cautions that "it would probably be a mistake to see the whole of *The Red Pony* as illustrating the rites of initiation step by step and in sequence," he points to Frazer's *The Golden Bough* as a source of what he sees as "a general pattern" of ancient puberty rites in the story cycle. Robert M. Benton claims that Lisca "stands almost alone among major critics as one who gives serious attention to the work [*The Red Pony*]." Benton complains rightly that "most do little more than call the novella a *Bildungsroman.*"[39]

It would be inaccurate to say that Jody Tiflin "becomes a man" in *The Red Pony*; Jody begins the first story as "only a little boy," and we are reminded at the beginning of each succeeding story that Jody is still only a little boy. Jody does not grow up in these stories morally or emotionally in any way comparable to Ike McCaslin in "The Bear" or Nick Adams in the Hemingway stories. The most we can find in Jody is a rather faint suggestion of moral growth in his expanding awareness of and understanding of death. In fact, *The Red Pony* does not fit neatly into the category of "initiation," even though Jody does grow in these stories and death is his principal teacher. Rather than simply illustrating "the first tortured question of 'why?' and the acceptance," the four stories chronicle a different kind of growth, the growing question within Jody not of "why" but of "what"—what lies back within the mysterious dark mountains and back within the unknowable mystery of death. Developing within the boy is the courage it will take to follow in the path of old Gitano, the paisano who confronts the western mountains and death in "The Gift," the first story in *The Red Pony* cycle. This is the courage upon which any future for Jody as a "leader of people" must be founded.

The theme of death is introduced early in "The Gift." From Jody's entrance and Steinbeck's statement that "he was only a little boy," we are made vividly aware that Jody lives in a world in which death is an omnipresent reality and in which, as in "Flight," the line between life and death is very tenuous. This idea is first suggested in the "spot of blood" which Jody scrapes from his breakfast egg. "That's only a sign the rooster leaves," Billy Buck tells Jody (p. 204). It is, in fact, a sign of a chicken that will not be hatched because of Jody's breakfast. We soon learn that Billy Buck and Carl Tiflin, Jody's father, are getting ready to take some old milk cows to the butcher, and we are told incidentally that Smasher, the shepherd, has killed a coyote and lost an ear doing so. The black cypress tree where the pigs are killed makes its first appearance at this point, and, in a foreshadowing of the red pony's fate,

Jody sees "two big black buzzards" circling over a nearby hill and is vaguely conscious that "some animal had died in the vicinity" (p. 206).

The opening pages of the story suggest that Jody's world is permeated by the presence of death. As yet, however, death exists for Jody as an impersonal force and even an enjoyable diversion, as his excitement over the possibility of pig killing suggests. In the course of the story, he will realize death as a personal and profound experience, and it will move from the periphery of his consciousness to implant itself deeply in his unconscious.

Once Carl and Billy have departed to sell the cows and purchase the pony (most likely with money from the slaughtered cows), references to and images of death disappear from the story as Jody becomes absorbed in the vibrant life-force of the red pony. Jody names the pony for the mountains of life, the Gabilans to the east across the Salinas Valley, and Billy Buck understands the connection: "Billy Buck knew how he felt." However, Steinbeck has insured that an awareness of death's imminence has been firmly planted in his readers' minds. And when the time comes for the pony to die, it struggles desperately away from the barn onto the slopes of the Santa Lucias, the western mountains, and, like Pepé in "Flight," falls prey to the buzzards. Thus, ironically, the power of death over life is asserted as "Gabilan Mountains" lies dying in the Santa Lucias.

What Jody has the opportunity to learn in this story is not only to accept the inevitability of death but to know death as a personal and profoundly disturbing experience. There is a suggestion that he is beginning to recognize death in a new way when, as Gabilan lies dying, he goes to the spring to meditate. While sitting at the spring, "he looked down at the dark cypress tree. The place was familiar, but curiously changed. It wasn't itself any more, but a frame for things that were happening" (p. 235). There is a suggestion that perhaps death is becoming personalized for Jody for the first time.

When Jody attacks the buzzard that has begun to feed on the dying pony, he looks as never before directly into the face of death: "His fingers found the neck of the struggling bird. The red eyes looked into his face, calm and fearless and fierce" (p. 238). And, as he batters the buzzard, we are told, "the red fearless eyes still looked at him, impersonal and unafraid and detached" (p. 238).

The gift to Jody in this first story has been much more than a pony. It has been a new awareness of the mystery and power of death. As becomes evident in the second story, "The Great Mountains," what Jody has gained has not been a new sense of the value or sacredness of life or a new sense of his responsibility to all life, but rather simply an awakened sense of wonder about the realm of death symbolized by the mountains.

The second story in *The Red Pony* begins by reminding us that we are still dealing with a young boy: "In the humming heat of a midsummer afternoon the little boy Jody listlessly looked about the ranch for something to do" (pp. 238–39). Lest we assume too much regarding the maturation that has taken place in the previous story, Steinbeck not only reminds us of Jody's immaturity, but immediately shows Jody irresponsibly destroying the swallows' "little mud houses" and cruelly tormenting "that good big dog," Doubletree Mutt. Next, Jody kills and dismembers a small bird, feeling "a little mean pain in his stomach" because he knew that the adults would disapprove of the deed.

Obviously, Gabilan's death has not taught Jody to value life or to act more responsibly toward that life. Morally, he seems not to have matured at all between the stories. However, after Jody has washed the blood from his hands in the spring, he sits and watches clouds sail over the western mountains, the "great mountains ... growing darker and more savage until they finished with one jagged ridge, high up against the west. Curious secret mountains; he thought of the little he knew about them" (p. 241). Jody is beginning to wonder about this mysterious country. He asks his father, "Has anybody been there?" and the answer is "A few people, I guess. It's dangerous." Carl Tiflin is a shortsighted man, absorbed in the work of the ranch, a man for whom the frightening mystery of the mountains is a danger simply to be avoided. Carl is content to repeat the dubious assertion that "there's more unexplored country in the mountains of Monterey County than any other place in the United States" (p. 241). Jody, on the contrary, shows the first promise of developing toward the future suggested in "The Leader of the People" when he says, "it would be good to go." And Steinbeck adds, "Jody knew something was there, something very wonderful because it wasn't known, something secret and mysterious" (p. 241).

The mysterious, unknown thing Jody senses in the mountains includes much to fear, for in the evening "when the sun had gone over the edge ... and the mountains were a purple-like despair, then Jody was afraid of them; then they were so impersonal and aloof that their very imperturbability was a threat" (p. 242). This cold imperturbability is possibly so frightening to Jody because he has encountered it once before as an important element in his first direct experience of death—in the "impersonal and unafraid and detached" eyes of the buzzard.

Jody has already identified the life-force of the red pony with the Gabilan Mountains, and here he instinctively contrasts the disturbing western mountains with the eastern Gabilans: "Now he turned his head toward the mountains of the east, the Gabilans, and they were jolly mountains, with hill ranches in their creases. ... He looked back for an instant at the Great Ones and shivered a little at the contrast" (p. 242). The two ranges of mountains stand as opposing symbols of life and death in this story, and Jody is being increasingly drawn toward the latter.

Richard F. Peterson has called this story "a strange and disturbing interlude in Steinbeck's portrait of the painful and sometimes violent education of the young boy."[40] Rather than being an interlude, however, this story illustrates the most central element in the moral awakening Jody undergoes in the course of the four stories. Here we see the blossoming of Jody's questing impulse, his desire to transcend the known and secure world of the Gabilans and the home ranch and to know what is ultimately unknowable. Already he has surpassed his father and even Billy Buck, who, like Carl, prefers not to think about the mountains. At this stage in the cycle, Steinbeck introduces Gitano, the aged Quester and bearer of the Grail, to augment this phase of Jody's education.

While it is difficult to agree completely with Peterson that Steinbeck introduces the "waste land theme" through mood and setting in this story, Peterson convincingly draws upon evidence from Weston's *From Ritual to Romance* to relate Gitano's rapier to the Grail legend. Peterson suggests that "the central event in the story which defines the roles of Gitano and Jody within the mythic pattern of the quest for the Grail is Jody's discovery of the 'lean and lovely rapier with a golden basket hilt.'" In Weston, Peterson notes evidence that "in many of the earlier forms of the Grail legend the Grail appears in juxtaposition with the Lance or Spear of Christ's passion," and suggests persuasively that Gitano's rapier may represent "this combination of Grail symbols."[41] Given Steinbeck's lifelong fascination with the Grail legend and the recurrent appearance of the quest motif in his writing, it seems likely that Peterson's interpretation is valid. However, of central importance here is not whether Gitano represents the "Maimed King" as Peterson asserts, with Jody as Quester. More important is Gitano's similarity to Joseph Wayne, Pepé Torres, and Kino. Like each of these other Steinbeck characters, Gitano represents the courage necessary to actively confront the mystery of death in the mountains. Like Joseph Wayne, Gitano expresses a deep commitment to place, returning to the place of his birth when it is time for him to die. Gitano is a version of the Grail Knight, bearing his shimmering rapier aloft as he rides off on the suggestively named horse, Old Easter, in quest of the unknowable.

Jody already has instinctively identified Gitano with the western mountains. "Did you come out of the mountains?" he asks upon first meeting the old man. And Steinbeck describes Jody's reaction to the old man: "Gitano was mysterious like the mountains. There were ranges back as far as you could see, but behind that last range against the sky there was a great unknown country. And Gitano was an old man, until you got to the dull dark eyes. And in behind them was some unknown thing" (p. 252). That unknown thing, like Hamlet's "undiscovered country," is death.

Typically, Carl Tiflin does not understand why Gitano has taken Old Easter and gone into the mountains. "I wonder what he wants back there," he says (p. 255). Jody, however, is much more sensitive to Gitano's purpose: "He looked searchingly at the mountains. . . . Jody thought of the rapier and of Gitano. And he thought of the great mountains. A longing caressed him, and it was so sharp that he wanted to cry to get it out of his breast. . . . and he was full of a nameless sorrow" (p. 256). Clifford Lawrence Lewis has suggested that Jody's "nameless sorrow" is "for the passing of a history and tradition that Gitano takes with him." Peter Lisca comes nearer the mark, however, when he asserts that Jody's sorrow comes "not from grief for Gitano or the old horse, but rather an emotional perception of that whole of which Gitano, Old Easter, the rapier, and the Great Mountains are parts, a recognition of the symbolic significance of their conjunction."[42] To be more specific, Jody's sorrow and his painful longing represent a more profound version of his earlier yearning to know what was back in the heart of the mountains. Instinctively, Jody recognizes that Gitano is riding off to meet his death and that he is not simply accepting it but actively seeking it; he is a questing knight. The emphasis is not on the simple fact that Gitano and the old horse will undoubtedly die in the mountains, but on the quest for that knowledge of man's relationship with the whole which, as it was for Joseph Wayne and Pepé Torres, is attainable in the mountains at the moment of death. We are shown here that Jody, a future "leader of the people," has a powerful questing impulse developing within him.

In contrast to the pervasive symbols of and references to death that permeate the beginning of "The Gift" and the conclusion of "The Great Mountains," "The Promise" opens in spring, the season of rebirth, or, as Steinbeck would later write in *The Wayward Bus*, of "flowering and growth." Again Jody is introduced as "the little boy, Jody," reminding us that regardless of what experiences have befallen Jody in the previous stories, he is still a child. Here, in fact, Jody seems younger than ever as he leads an imaginary army home from school and surprises his mother with a lunch pail full of smothered reptiles and insects. The spring is vibrant: "The afternoon was green and gold with spring. Underneath the spread branches of the oaks the plants grew pale and tall, and on the hills the feed was smooth and thick" (p. 256).

In this season of rebirth, Jody's father allows Jody to take the mare, Nellie, to be bred, promising that Jody may have the colt to raise when it is born. In this story Jody learns with harsh brutality the interrelatedness of life and death when Billy Buck must finally kill Nellie to save the colt and fulfill his promise to the boy. In "The Promise," Jody's vague yearning to fathom the mysteries of death represented by Gitano and the mysterious mountains is partially fulfilled. After Billy delivers the colt from the dying mare, Jody learns a new lesson: "He tried to be glad because of the colt, but the bloody face, and the haunted, tired eyes of Billy Buck hung in the air ahead of him" (p. 279). In "The Gift" Jody experienced death for the first time as a personal but uncontrollable force which must simply be accepted. In "The Great Mountains" he became aware of the courage involved in accepting one's own death and going out to confront that "unknown thing" in the mountains. In "The Promise" he watches as Billy Buck goes beyond acceptance and makes the decision as to which shall live, Nellie or the colt.

Lisca suggests that "the mare's suffering and death are the price of life and give to Jody a new sense of his responsibility to that life." Lewis states that "by compressing the time between birth and death, Steinbeck has managed to intimately connect the birth and death process."[43] While the birth of the colt certainly does provide Jody with a powerful lesson in the intimate connection between life and death, and while he is unquestionably impressed by the death of the mare, what Jody learns here is more than "a new sense of responsibility to . . . life." Nor does the lesson merely underscore the important theme of the interrelatedness of life and death. Jody's real lesson is provided by Billy Buck, by the "haunted, tired eyes" that "hung in the air ahead of him" as he tried to think only of the new colt. Rather than a new respect for life, Jody has a deeper understanding of what it means to challenge death instead of merely accepting its inevitability.

If Jody had indeed learned to value life more greatly, or to view death more maturely as a serious and integral part of that life which one must respect, we should expect to see a far different boy in the final story of *The Red Pony*, a boy vastly different from the one who casually destroyed the swallows' nests or mutilated the bird or exulted in the possibility of pig killing. We should, in short, expect to meet a Jody who has a much more mature respect for the principle of life in "The Leader of the People."

When we do meet Jody in this final story, added to the first three stories in the 1945 publication of *The Red Pony*, he is introduced as usual as "the little boy, Jody" (p. 283). Almost immediately, in this story, we see Jody rejoicing in the potential slaughter of the mice: "Jody sighed with satisfaction. Those plump, sleek, arrogant mice were doomed. For eight months they had lived and multiplied in the haystack. They had been immune from cats, from traps, from poison and from Jody. They had grown smug in their security, overbearing and fat. Now the time of disaster had come; they would not survive another day" (p. 284). Death in this final story is once again a part of the play world of Jody Tiflin; we get no indication of a new sense of responsibility toward life in Jody here. When Jody tries to please Grandfather by suggesting that there may be a pig killing, we seem to be right back where we started in "The Gift" as far as Jody's attitude toward death is concerned.

The pattern of the four stories in *The Red Pony* is to present a stark, personal encounter with death in the first story and to follow this with a more abstract experience of death in the second. The third story then introduces a second harsh, immediate experience of death, and the fourth provides another encounter with abstract values. The final story, "The Leader of the People," is about the questing impulse that is at the core of what Grandfather terms "westering"—the American migration from the Atlantic to the Pacific. Grandfather serves as a second type of Quester in the book, both similar to and very different from Gitano. Grandfather has led a wagon train to California and run into the barrier of the Pacific Ocean. He is caught up in the archetypal American westward movement, trapped in it. For Grandfather, "once made, no step could ever be retraced; once headed in a direction, the path would never bend nor the pace increase or slow" (pp. 290–91). As Jody's mother says, "if there'd been any farther west to go, he'd have gone." She adds, "He lives right by the ocean where he had to stop," and Carl Tiflin comments, "I've seen him. . . . He goes down and stares off west over the ocean" (p. 288). Grandfather is one of the pathetic old men he himself describes, lined up "along the shore hating the ocean because it stopped them" (p. 302). He encapsulates the westward movement, a microcosm of that phase of American history. "It was westering and westering," Grandfather tells Jody; "it wasn't getting here that mattered, it was movement and westering" (p. 302).

Caught up in the westering pattern, Grandfather represents one aspect of the Quester—the desire to know what is unknown, what is beyond the horizon. West is the direction of the setting sun and death, as Steinbeck suggested in *To a God Unknown*, where another old man lived right by the ocean attempting to worship that which he could not know. Grandfather is similar to Gitano in that, like the old paisano, he yearns to experience what has not been experienced, to continue the quest indefinitely. In a more important sense, however, Grandfather is involved in a much less significant and less meaningful quest than Gitano's. While Gitano demonstrated both commitment to place and the courage to explore the inner consciousness symbolized by the "unknown thing" Jody sensed within Gitano's eyes, Grandfather's quest is wholly outward and away from commitment. Grandfather is in a perpetual state of running away from commitment. When Jody suggests, "Maybe I could lead the people someday," Grandfather replies, "There's no place to go. There's the ocean to stop you." Jody says, "In boats I might, sir," and Grandfather insists, "No place to go, Jody. Every place is taken. But that's not the worst. . . . Westering has died out of the people. Westering isn't a hunger any more" (p. 303). As a serious reader of Jung, Weston, and Frazer and an acquaintance of Joseph Campbell, Steinbeck was acutely aware of the sea as a symbol of death and the unconscious—an awareness that is amply illustrated in the war dispatches he wrote in 1945, the same year as the publication of *The Red Pony* in book form.[44] The fact that it is Jody who is eager to venture into this new unknown region, whether it be the mountains or sea, suggests that he may become a greater Quester than Grandfather, that he may one day demonstrate the courage and commitment of Gitano.

Jody's sympathy for Grandfather at the end of "The Leader of the People" indicates that Jody recognizes the futility of Grandfather's predicament, that of one who cannot rest yet is confronted by a barrier he cannot surmount. Whatever promise Jody shows in this story depends upon his own incipient questing instinct, one that may allow him to move beyond the westering pattern to explore more significant territories. Jody has demonstrated no greater sensitivity to the value of life than he had in the first story; the mice may be spared for a while out of deference to Grandfather but they will most likely perish under Jody's flail another day.

Steinbeck will later recreate the westward migration in *The Grapes of Wrath*, and in so doing, he will attempt to cast off the values inherent in the westering tradition represented by Grandfather. As *To a God Unknown* demonstrated, Steinbeck's emphasis is on commitment to place and on man's understanding of his relationship to the "whole" of which he is a part. The pattern of noncommitment illustrated by the westering impulse in American history is in direct contrast to and a contradiction of the values Steinbeck asserts throughout his writing. Grandfather, unlike Gitano, is not a hero; he is simply one of the pathetic old men. He cannot and will not turn back to explore the country he has found; he will not *know* his place in the whole, for he lacks the kind of commitment demonstrated by Joseph Wayne and Gitano and suggested in Jody.

Notes

38. Steinbeck, "My Short Novels," *Wings*, October 1953, p. 4.

39. Arnold L. Goldsmith, "Thematic Rhythm in *The Red Pony*," in *Steinbeck: A Collection of Critical Essays*, ed. Robert Murray Davis (Englewood Cliffs, N.J.: Prentice-Hall, 1972), pp. 72, 70; Fontenrose, *John Steinbeck: An Introduction and Interpretation*, p. 64; Lisca, *Wide World of Steinbeck*, p. 10; Robert M. Benton, "Realism, Growth, and Contrast in 'The Gift,'" *Steinbeck Quarterly* 6 (Winter 1973): 3.

40. Richard F. Peterson, "The Grail Legend and Steinbeck's 'The Great Mountains,'" *Steinbeck Quarterly* 6 (Winter 1973): 9.

41. Ibid., pp. 12, 13.

42. Clifford Lawrence Lewis, "John Steinbeck: Architect of the Unconscious" (Ph.D. diss., University of Texas at Austin, 1972), p. 104; Peter Lisca, *John Steinbeck: Nature and Myth* (New York: Thomas Y. Crowell, 1975), p. 198.

43. Lisca, *Wide World of Steinbeck*, p. 103; Lewis, "John Steinbeck: Architect of the Unconscious," p. 106.

44. Robert DeMott cites Steinbeck's relationship with Campbell in "Toward a Redefinition of *To a God Unknown*." For a discussion of Steinbeck's war dispatches, see my essay "The Threshold of War: Steinbeck's Quest in *Once There Was a War*," *Steinbeck Quarterly* 13, nos. 3–4 (1980): 80–86.

JOHN H. TIMMERMAN

The Red Pony: *"The Desolation of Loss"*

When in February 1932 the firm reorganized as Jonathan Cape and Robert Ballou, Inc., issued a contract for *The Pastures of Heaven*, it also signed the next two novels Steinbeck produced: "There are three contracts, one for The Pastures of Heaven and one each for two later mss which are simply named by their succession. The publisher binds himself to publish the things sight unseen" (*SLL*, p. 61). Although the Great Depression was about to make these "binding" promises little more than dreams, the rare praise spurred Steinbeck's work. His first action was typical for a writer: What do I have on hand? The unwieldy carcass of *To a God Unknown* had been lying around in unsettled stages for several years. For the first half of 1932, Steinbeck again wrestled with the manuscript to prepare it for publication.

By mid-1932, however, his mind was running to other stories he wanted to tell. In June 1932, Robert Ballou, now with the firm of Brewer, Warren and Putnam, requested biographical data to be used for publicity. For Steinbeck, the request evoked memories of the past and his personal stories. He was still hovering between writing of the people and places he knew, as in *The Pastures of Heaven*, and writing of the great mythic concepts that fired his imagination, as in *To a God Unknown*. The request pointed a direction, and Steinbeck reflected in reply,

From *The Dramatic Landscape of Steinbeck's Short Stories*, pp. 117–39, 299–302. Copyright © 1990 by the University of Oklahoma Press.

Immediately there arises a problem of emphasis. Things of the greatest emphasis to me would be more or less meaningless to anyone else. Such a biography would consist of such things as— the way the sparrows hopped about on the mud street early in the morning when I was little—how the noon bell sounded when we were writing dirty words on the sidewalk with red fuchsia berries— how Teddy got run over by a fire engine, and the desolation of loss—the most tremendous morning in the world when my pony had a cold. [*SLL*, pp. 62–63]

For the first time, the possibility of the story of the red pony arises. With it arose his greatest challenge of a writer: making those "things of greatest emphasis to me" and perhaps "meaningless to anyone else" meaningful to anyone else by the alchemy of art.

By early January 1933, Steinbeck had finished work on *To a God Unknown* and was now looking for a new subject. In a letter to Mavis McIntosh, he lists in remarkable detail a series of possible short stories. Each of them evolves directly from his own past. Writing them, however, was stalled by the sudden illness of Steinbeck's mother in March 1933. Paralyzed by a massive stroke, she was hospitalized until June when she returned to the family house on Central Avenue, where John, as the only child free from the rigors of a regular job, moved to tend her. There he began writing the *Red Pony* stories, living once more in his childhood home and tending his ill mother and increasingly bewildered father. The reversion to the childhood stories of Jody, as Jackson Benson points out, "gains an extra measure of poignancy when placed within the circumstances of its composition."[1]

Steinbeck wrote George Albee at this time, "I have the pony story about half written. I like it pretty well. It is more being written for discipline than for any other reason. I mean if I can write any kind of a story at a time like this, then I can write 'stories'" (*SLL*, p. 71). He goes on to describe the action and style of the first story:

It is a very simple story about a boy who gets a colt pony and the pony gets distemper. There is a good deal in it, first about the training of horses and second about the treatment of distemper. This may not seem like a good basis for a story but that entirely depends upon the treatment. The whole thing is as simply told as though it came out of the boy's mind although there is no going into the boy's mind. It is an attempt to make the reader create the boy's mind for himself. An interesting experiment you see if nothing else. [*SLL*, p. 71]

The backdrop of a confrontation with his own past while living again in the family home, the prolonged dying of his mother, and the recollection of childhood provide a rich thematic context for these stories. They are very much about the realization of lost youth, maturity through understanding of death, and the loss of innocence.

The writing itself was anything but an easy passage. Fractured by incessant demands, it seemed an erratic diversion rather than a concentrated effort. Steinbeck recounts the effort in a letter to Albee:

> The pony story, you can understand has been put off for a while. But now I spend about seven hours a day in the hospital and I am trying to go on with it, but with not a great deal of success, because partly I have to fight an atmosphere of blue fog so thick and so endless that I can see no opening in it. However, if I can do it, it will be good. Anyone can write when the situation is propitious. [*SLL*, p. 73]

A few days later he again wrote Albee, this time telling how he was trying to type the second draft of the story while being constantly interrupted to tend his mother: "One paragraph—help lift patient on bed pan. Back, a little ill, three paragraphs, help turn patient so sheets can be changed" (*SLL*, p. 83). Steinbeck made a poor nurse. He openly confessed to a "fear and hatred of illness and incapacity which amounts to a mania" (*SLL*, p. 83) and often returned to the typewriter feeling nauseated and emotionally drained. Yet, the story developed steadily and deliberately.

This period also marked the growth of Steinbeck's intense interest in his phalanx theory. In a June 21, 1933, letter to Carlton Sheffield, Steinbeck relates the group organism concept to his mother's illness: "Half of the cell units of my mother's body have rebelled. Neither has died, but the devolution has changed her functions. That is cruel to say. . . . She, as a human unit, is deterred from functioning as she ordinarily did by a schism of a number of her cells" (*SLL*, p. 76). He also announces that "when the parts of this thesis have found their places, I'll start trying to put them into the symbolism of fiction."

At this point, in June, Steinbeck had not yet seen a link between the *Red Pony* stories and the phalanx. Having finished writing "The Gift" in late June 1933, he wrote, "It was good training in self control and that's about all the good it is. Now I have my new theme to think about there will be a few loopholes in my days. I can think about it while helping with a bed pan" (p. 78). Steinbeck's intention with the stories was to keep them narratively pure, free from the philosophical burden that weighed down *To a God Unknown*: "It is an unpretentious story. I think the philosophic content is so buried that it will not bother anybody" (*SLL*, p. 85). Nonetheless, as the writing continued over the summer of 1933 and the phalanx ideas developed simultaneously, if largely through his correspondence, one begins to observe an overlap between the two. There are huge, amorphous patterns in this life that one cannot fully control, that seem to develop a force and life of their own. One such pattern is death itself. How we deal with the force, submitting blindly to it or battling against it and maturing through it, determines our own place in life.

The stories were also a bit like a phalanx, acquiring a life of their own that forged steadily onward. Writing continued into the fall of 1933, when Steinbeck started the first writing on Tortilla Flat in the notebook containing some of the *Red Pony* stories. The *Tortilla Flat* draft, with the central character identified as Bennie, then Benny, covers roughly eighty pages of the ledger in a complete draft. The "Beans and Tortillas" story of Señora Terrasina Cortez follows, to be incorporated into the revised novel, then the first draft of "The Murder" and several drafts of "The Chrysanthemums."[2] At the end of the ledger, in early 1934, Steinbeck returned again to the *Red Pony* stories.

By May 1934, now working in the ledger notebook that would contain stories for *The Long Valley*, Steinbeck had apparently exhausted the *Red Pony* stories. He announces,

> I think I'll get to some short stories. I feel that I should be able to do one story a week. In two or three months I would have enough for a volume or more and maybe it could come out. I don't know. But I must work like a dog. I do know that. And why not after all. There's no reason why if I do my work every day—see few people, think, walk some, I shouldn't get a good series out. Things are ticking along in my head all ready." [*LVN*]

He comments that he had written five stories of "Jody, or in which Jody was the eyes." The fifth story, if it was written, has not survived. Perhaps the fifth existed only in Steinbeck's mind, for following the note he outlines a *Red Pony* story in which Jody and his mother go to church, Carl Tiflin having refused to accompany them. Apparently the story would test matters of belief versus pragmatism, focusing upon Jody and his mother's seeing a ghost. Carl, who has little patience for either the imagination or faith, rejects the experience. In Carl's view, it is against "the law," and for him the law is the world of pragmatic reality. But Steinbeck cut the outline short:

> After all, why should I go on with the stories of Jody—forced stories. I have two of them in New York now. If they want more,

I'll send them when they've used up what I sent. Meanwhile why shouldn't I write some for a possibly more expensive market. There's nothing holding me to these stories save an apparent willingness on the part of the magazine to buy them. Let's do something else for a change then. Something more to liking. Something it isn't necessary to force. That shouldn't be too hard. I know, I'll tell the story of the raid in Watsonville. [*LVN*]

Apparently, the stories were finished as a series, and his attention turned to the new activity of the stories that would eventually comprise *The Long Valley*. They did, however, open the door to a paying market. By the end of the summer of 1933, McIntosh and Otis had placed two of the *Red Pony* stories, "The Gift" and "The Great Mountains," with *North American Review*, a periodical with a limited circulation but excellent prestige. They appeared in the November 1933 and December 1933 issues. Subsequently, the periodical purchased three additional stories, "The Murder," "The White Quail," and "The Raid" for between forty-five and fifty dollars each. "The Promise," written in the winter of 1934, was turned down for publication by the *North American Review* but was eventually published in *Harper's Magazine* in August 1937. "The Leader of the People," written in late winter or early spring of 1934, was first published in the British periodical *Argosy* in August 1936.

Written during a period of acute psychological duress, the *Red Pony* stories have a richness of narrative texture and theme that has made them a treasured addition to anthologies and a treasure trove to critics. They possess a belying simplicity of tone and point of view, but one that is extremely difficult to capture fictionally. The contrast between the youthful innocence of Jody and the pragmatic vision of his elders has made the stories enduring favorites at the high-school level. The forceful grappling with death and the rich stylistic qualities have enamored scholars.

Accepting Steinbeck's fundamental premise of a young boy's initiatory experiences, several critics have divided that experience into psychological categories. Joseph Fontenrose views the story as a "passage from naive childhood to the threshold of adulthood through knowledge of birth, old age, and death, gained through experience with horses," the whole of which he likens to Faulkner's "The Bear."[3] Joseph Warren Beach likens it to Marjorie Rawlings's *The Yearling*,[4] and Arnold Goldsmith observes a resemblance to Hemingway's Nick Adams stories.[5] The comparison with Hemingway is also developed by Mimi Gladstein in her analysis of Jody's growing into a "person," which she signifies by use of the Yiddish word "mensch."[6] In order to focus the initiation pattern, R. Baird Shuman applies the framework of Mircea Eliade's *Rites and Symbols of Initiation* to the story.[7]

Several studies have explored symbolic properties of the tales. Frederic I. Carpenter suggests that "the red pony is also the physical symbol of the old American dream,"[8] a view that Peter Lisca deemed "possible by simplifications amounting to distortion."[9] In their exchange on the idea of westering in "The Leader of the People," Donald E. Houghton and Robert E. Morsberger demonstrate that the American dream motif is, at least, very much an issue in the final tale.[10] In his study "The Black Cypress and the Green Tub: Death and Procreation in Steinbeck's 'The Promise,'" Robert S. Hughes, Jr., argues that there is a great deal more symbolism in the stories that we observe by a casual reading.[11] His study is one of the few to provide a lucid explication of their patterns of imagery.

All these permutations of the scholarly mind are certainly important to a full appreciation of the work. As Hamlet said, "There are more things in heaven and earth, Horatio, / Than are dreamt of in your philosophy," so too any artist crafts more patterns into his work than he is consciously aware of. It is also true, as Warren French observes, that "Steinbeck was a more self-conscious narrative architect than has always been recognized, but even he in his cyclical works, like *The Pastures of Heaven, Cannery Row,* and *The Red Pony,* created more subtle patterns than he may have deliberately contemplated in providing an overall meaning for seemingly heterogeneous elements in an episodic narrative."[12]

While standing independently of each other, the *Red Pony* stories share an organic structural unity as a whole through several patterns. The first of these is a natural time progression beginning in Jody's tenth year and ending in his twelfth. "The Gift" begins in late August, with the start of the school year, and concludes with Gabilan's death shortly before Thanksgiving, at the start of the rainy winter season. "The Great Mountains" begins in midsummer of the following year, and the entire story covers less than twenty-four hours. The rage that Jody vents at the end of "The Gift" by smashing a buzzard's head carries over to the beginning of "The Great Mountains," when he kills a thrush with a stone and cuts off the bird's head. "The Gift" ends with Jody smeared with the blood from the buzzard; in "The Great Mountains," Jody "drank from the mossy tub and washed the bird's blood from his hands in cold water" (p. 240).[13]

"The Promise" begins in the spring of the following year and ends on February 2 with the death of Nellie and the birth of the black colt. "The Leader of the People" begins in the spring, when Billy Buck rakes together "the last of the old year's haystack." The stories, then, follow an annual cycle, covering events in two years of the life of Jody Tiflin.

Other subtle patterns lend a structured unity to the whole. While the first story begins at daybreak, suggesting the youth and innocence of Jody, subsequent stories begin on "a midsummer afternoon," "mid-afternoon of spring," and a "Saturday afternoon." The rhythmical pattern may be extended, as Arnold L. Goldsmith observes in "Thematic Rhythm in *The Red Pony*": "Steinbeck follows the violence of the first story with the tragic quiet of the second, with this same pattern repeated in the third and fourth sections. Where the first and third stories are about the violent deaths of horses, the second and fourth are about the twilight years of two old men."[14] The entire pattern, Goldsmith points out, represents "the neverending rhythm of life and death to which Jody is continually exposed."[15]

Throughout the cycle of changes, however, Steinbeck persistently identifies Jody, at the beginning of each story, as a youth. In "The Gift" we meet him as "only a little boy, ten years old, with hair like yellow grass and with shy polite gray eyes, and with a mouth that worked when he thought" (p. 202). In subsequent stories he is introduced each time, as "the little boy Jody." Thus the larger theme emerges: A little boy is finding his place in the larger rhythmical patterns of life and death, of passing time, of dreams and responsibilities.

Steinbeck made his thematic intentions for *The Red Pony* quite clear. In addition to the notes and letters of the time, we have a remarkably candid retrospective statement in "My Short Novels":

> *The Red Pony* was written a long time ago, when there was desolation in my family. The first death occurred. And the family, which every child believes to be immortal, was shattered. Perhaps this is the first adulthood of any man or woman. The first tortured question "Why?" and then acceptance, and then the child becomes a man. *The Red Pony* was an attempt, an experiment if you wish, to set down this loss and acceptance and growth.[16]

The pattern of "loss and acceptance and growth" furnishes the basic theme for the tales and culminates very successfully in the much-disputed "Leader of the People."

The maturation of Jody is developed in several minor patterns that complement and sustain the major pattern of the experience of death. The most notable of these is the relationship with his father, Carl. From the start Carl Tiflin demonstrates three qualities that provide a framework for Jody's adolescent spirit of rebellion: stern discipline, incipient cruelty, and pragmatic realism.

A stern, unbending man, Carl possesses a rigid sense of ordered discipline. This is all that Jody has known—an unyielding framework of rules. He obeys his father "in everything without questions of any kind" (p. 203). Rules are produced by Carl with the aim of order, but also of training Jody to his high sense of dignity. Thus, he suspects Jody's own careful training of Gabilan because it might produce a "trick horse." Watching Gabilan working on the long halter, Carl observes, "He's getting to be almost a trick pony. . . . I don't like trick horses. It takes all the—dignity out of a horse to make him do tricks. Why, a trick horse is kind of like an actor—no dignity, no character of his own" (pp. 217–18). What Carl fails to see is the association between Gabilan's training and his own training of Jody. It has never occurred to him that his own rigid discipline threatens Jody's independence, almost transforming him into a trick boy. So it is also that Jody's sense of revolt at Carl's rules becomes closely allied with Gabilan's spirit, for Jody is very much a young boy in rebellion, finding his own ways to assert his independence. Walking through the vegetable garden, "He paused for a moment to smash a green muskmelon with his heel, but he was not happy about it. It was a bad thing to do, he knew perfectly well" (p. 205). This minor act of defiance is a part of the general rebellion at the start of the school year: "There was still a spirit of revolt among the pupils" (p. 206). Jody's independent spirit is mirrored in Gabilan, whose eyes shine with "the light of disobedience."

Carl's character is marked by a kind of aloof and stern dignity, but he can also be a cruel man. His incipient cruelty is openly manifested with old Gitano. While hating the brutality he shows to Gitano, he nonetheless turns on the old man:

> "It's a shame not to shoot Easter," he said. "It'd save him a lot of pains and rheumatism." He looked secretly at Gitano, to see whether he noticed the parallel, but the big bony hands did not move, nor did the dark eyes turn from the horse. "Old things ought to be put out of their misery," Jody's father went on. "One shot, a big noise, one big pain in the head maybe, and that's all. That's better than stiffness and sore teeth." [p. 249]

The cruelty carries to Grandfather as well, for here too is an "old thing" that ought to be put out of his misery. Ironically, Carl's own cruelty defeats him. Thinking that Grandfather is out of earshot, Carl berates the old man mercilessly. Terribly shamed by his outburst, Carl stalks out of the kitchen, but Jody has witnessed the unraveling of his father's stern dignity:

> Jody glanced in shame at his mother, and he saw that she was looking at Carl, and that she wasn't breathing. It was an awful thing that he was doing. He was tearing himself to pieces to talk like that. It was a terrible thing to him to retract a word, but to retract it in shame was infinitely worse. [p. 301]

The tyrannical order of sternness has crumbled, and in its wreckage Jody comes of age. With his father's harshness shattered by shame, and bearing in mind Carl's attitude toward "old things" as worthless clutter, Jody steps into the role that rightfully should be Carl's.[17] Having lost heart for the gratuitous violence of killing the mice in the haystack, Jody ushers Grandfather into the house and makes him a glass of lemonade, the right action toward an old thing whose only sin has been to run out of room for his great dream of westering. Jody becomes the leader of the party.

To describe Carl Tiflin in such a way is not to imply that he is a mean or malicious man. Indeed, many readers have assumed that because he is the foil for Jody's maturation and for the key role-reversal in "The Leader of the People," Carl is something of the villain in the story. Billy Buck, in this view, operates as surrogate father to the boy, providing nurture and understanding. It would be more accurate, however, to characterize Carl as a victim of his own pragmatic concerns. Twice before the climactic shaming before Grandfather, he has his own attempts at capturing some larger vision thwarted. When Gabilan is dying, Carl attempts to cheer Jody by telling stories:

> He told about the wild man who ran naked through the country and had a tail and ears like a horse and he told about the rabbit-cats of Moro Cojo that hopped into the trees for birds. He revived the famous Maxwell brothers who found a vein of gold and hid the traces of it so carefully that they could never find it again. [p. 229]

Asking for some response from the silent, withdrawn Jody, Carl reacts with hurt and anger. He has no other resources. The scene foreshadows "The Leader of the People," wherein Carl himself ignores Grandfather's stories.

In "The Great Mountains," after cruelly demeaning Gitano, Carl again feels remorse: "Jody sat and secretly watched his father. He knew how mean his father felt" (p. 251). In this instance, Carl has failed to participate in Gitano's vision of a transcendent power in life, again foreshadowing his reaction to Grandfather. Stern he may be, even cruel at times, but Carl Tiflin represents nothing quite so much as a pragmatic authority locked in a prison of his own making.

"The Leader of the People," which brings the conflict between Jody and Carl to a culmination, gave Steinbeck considerably more difficulty than the other *Red Pony* stories. He seemed to want a sense of closure to the tales and to the thematic pattern of Jody's revolt and Carl's sternness. In an early draft the focus of the conflict centered upon the haystack, which served as an omen of tragedy:

> From the very first the haystack in the lower field was ill fated. In July when the pole was set up and the loaded header had creaked

up beside it, the big Jackson fork slipped and drove a tine through Billy Buck's foot. The little boy Jody watched Billy pull off his shoe and pour blood out of it, and jerk off his sock to prevent the poisoning of black dye. Billy was laid up then. Jody himself led the horse that pulled the Jackson fork tackle. At last the tall yellow stack was made and Jody's father thatched it carefully to keep the rain water out. That very afternoon Jody slid down the stack a few times and ruined the thatching so that it had to be done over again. This piece of badness on Jody's part not only brought instant punishment but had a far-reaching and sharp effect on the following Christmas for Jody's father Carl Tiflin was an irreparable punisher [last two words blurred]. [*TFN*]

The scene sets a conflict between Carl and Jody Tiflin, but it also depicts Jody as still a very immature child, rambunctious to be sure, but also willfully destructive for his own pleasure. It lacks the sense of growth Steinbeck had been aiming at.

In a second start to the story, under the title of "Grandfather," Steinbeck begins with Jody's being punished in school for shooting a needle through a reed blowgun into the woodwork around the blackboard. The teacher treats the offense promptly, but with a certain degree of lightness. This scene leads into the revised haystack scene, in which Carl catches him sliding down the haystack: "This piece of badness not only brought an instant punishment but had a far-reaching effect on the following Christmas, for Jody's father Carl Tiflin was a stern punisher and a keeper of his threats." The same conflict is there, and we never do learn the effect on the following Christmas. In this version, however, Jody vents his anger at being punished upon the mice in the haystack: "Those sleek, fat, smug mice who had lived all winter in the warm hay stack were good objects of revenge for all the evil of the stack. And Billy Buck had said the moldy straw was fairly crawling with fat frightened mice. Jody licked his nervous lips."

The mice hunt, which had appeared in bits and pieces throughout the ledger, exists in the final version only as a great expectancy.[18] But when the moment arrives, right after Carl's shame, Jody doesn't feel the same vengeful urge. Instead he gives up the hunt to wait upon Grandfather. Rebellion and vengeance are thereby replaced by a loving act of service. The full significance of Jody's bestowal of an act of grace upon Grandfather, however, is revealed in Jody's knowledge of death and Grandfather's great dream of westering, a pattern carefully and artistically developed in the work.

If, as Steinbeck so often commented, the *Red Pony* stories were an escape from the pressing reality of his mother's illness, the artistic discipline marking these stories is the more remarkable. The tales contain some of Steinbeck's finest, most carefully controlled descriptive passages to date, especially in the detailed portrayal of setting. The landscape of the Tiflin ranch emerges in crisply detailed portraits, seen by impressionistic snatches through Jody's eyes:

> On the fences the shiny blackbirds with red epaulets clicked their dry call. The meadowlarks sang like water, and the wild doves, concealed among the bursting leaves of the oaks, made a sound of restrained grieving. In the fields the rabbits sat sunning themselves, with only their forked ears showing above the grass heads. [pp. 262–63]

Steinbeck is not so much inventing as remembering in such passages; these are his foothills. Such descriptions rivet the landscape in sterling portraits.

The same use of intimate details characterizes Jody and make his youthfulness believable. The boy isn't precious; indeed, his humanity is seen in his relentless mistreatment of the enduring Doubletree Mutt, as fine a character as has limped through any of Steinbeck's stories and a testament to his lifelong affection for dogs. In a sense, Doubletree serves as the convenient displacement for Jody's revolt under his father's rules. But Jody isn't a mean sort; his world is an imaginative, if sometimes lonely one:

> Banging his knee against the golden lard bucket he used for school lunch, he contrived a good bass drum, while his tongue fluttered sharply against his teeth to fill in snare drums and occasional trumpets. Some time back the other members of the squad that walked so smartly from the school had turned into the various little canyons and taken the wagon roads to their own home ranches. Now Jody marched seemingly alone, with high-lifted knees and pounding feet; but behind him there was a phantom army with great flags and swords, silent but deadly. [p. 256]

In such portraits, Steinbeck reveals the imaginative quality of Jody that makes him more receptive to the mysteriousness of death and that opposes him to Carl's pragmatic rigidity.

In addition to his precise descriptions of a boy's world and his ability to capture Jody's youthful spirit, Steinbeck admits us to Jody's world through the eyes of others. News of Gabilan's arrival infects the schoolhouse boys with wonder, and Jody suddenly appears huge and marvelous before their eyes:

> Before today Jody had been a boy, dressed in overalls and a blue shirt—quieter than most, even suspected of being a little cowardly.

And now he was different. Out of a thousand centuries they drew the ancient admiration of the footman for the horseman. They knew instinctively that a man on a horse is spiritually as well as physically bigger than a man on foot. They knew that Jody had been miraculously lifted out of equality with them, and had been placed over them. [pp. 211–12]

While the boys traipse home in awestruck wonder, it is Jody who is left with the work of currying and brushing Gabilan. His wonder is vested in the pony itself.

The care of horses leads also to the care of Grandfather. On the one hand, this care of Gabilan and then Nellie results from Carl's dictates. Carl, who believes it is good discipline to give presents with reservations, adjures Jody to care for Gabilan: "If I ever hear of you not feeding him or leaving his stall dirty, I'll sell him off in a minute" (p. 209). When he decides to breed Nellie, once again Carl admonishes Jody: "You'll have to take care of her, too, till she throws the colt" (p. 260). But Carl's "care" is the rigid code of discipline unaffected by the emotions of the heart. Precisely those stirrings of the heart lead Jody to care for Grandfather after Carl shames him.

Jody is also touched by a sense of the mystical dream that places him closer to Grandfather's vision of westering than Carl. Carl's line of imagination seldom stretches beyond his own land, possibly as far as a sale in Salinas. He is the harsh, pragmatic man, incapable of dreaming. While less successful as a farmer, he is a bit like Raymond Banks, incapable of an imaginative world, and therefore impatient with Grandfather's great vision of westering. But from the outset, Jody has a keen sense of the transcendent vision.

Three great visionary dreams appear in the sequence of the tales, united by the mystical lure of the mountains and threading together the boy Jody, the dying Gitano, and the aged Grandfather. Each of them senses, in his own way, the power in life that transcends pragmatic reality, even mortality. One line of maturation in Jody is in the deepening sensitivity toward and appreciation for that mystical sense.

In "The Gift" Jody has fears for the welfare of his colt, the kind of childish nightmares that persist even into the waking vision. But these fears are described by Steinbeck as "a strong and a mysterious journey, to Jody—an extension of a dream" (p. 214). At this point he has no personal experience of life and death, simply feeling its dialectic as a raw possibility, a gray threat. At the end of the story, with Gabilan ill, Jody's sleep is disrupted as "the breathy groans of the pony sounded in his dreams" (p. 232). It is after the death of Gabilan, at the beginning of "The Great Mountains," that Jody first senses the mystical transcendence of vision, rather than merely dreaming. Lying on his back on a hill, Jody seems lifted toward the mountains. He squints his eyes, varying perspective. In a passage reminiscent of Gertie in "Fingers of Cloud," Steinbeck describes the experience:

> By closing one eye and destroying perspective he brought them down within reach so that he could put up his fingers and stroke them. He helped the gentle wind push them down the sky; it seemed to him that they went faster for his help. One fat white cloud he helped clear to the mountain rims and pressed it firmly over, out of sight. Jody wondered what it was seeing, then. He sat up the better to look at the great mountains where they went piling back, growing darker and more savage until they finished with one jagged ridge, high up against the west. Curious secret mountains; he thought of the little he knew about them. [p. 240]

The vision sets up the dialectic of the great mountains in the story, this geographical antithesis between the bright, mystical Gabilans and the darker, foreboding Santa Lucia range. Jody feels the mystic pull of the life-holding Gabilans: "They were jolly mountains, with hill ranches in their creases, and with pine trees growing on the crests" (p. 242). He fears the western Santa Lucia range with its strange, dark pull upon his spirit: "In the evening . . . the mountains were a purple-like despair, then Jody was afraid of them; then they were so impersonal and aloof that their very imperturbability was a threat" (p. 242). The paired ranges operate metaphorically here, as they would often in Steinbeck's work. In *East of Eden*, he recollects his own experience of the mountains in words that echo *The Red Pony*:

> I remember that the Gabilan Mountains to the east of the valley were light gay mountains full of sun and loveliness and a kind of invitation, so that you wanted to climb into the lap of a beloved mother. They were beckoning mountains with a brown grass love. The Santa Lucias stood up against the sky to the west and kept the valley from the open sea, and they were dark and brooding— unfriendly and dangerous. I always found in myself a dread of west and a love of east.[19]

Jody finds himself juxtaposed between, puzzled by, and finding his way through the contrary pulls of light and dark, life and death.

Having experienced the terror of death in Gabilan, Jody is tutored in the meaning of death and mystical transcendence by old Gitano: "Gitano was mysterious like the mountains. There were ranges back as far as you could see, but behind the last range piled up against the sky there was a great unknown country. And Gitano was an old man, until you got to the dull dark eyes. And in behind them was some unknown thing" (p. 252). When Jody had asked Carl what lay beyond the mountains, Carl answered in pragmatic terms: more mountains, cliffs, and brush and rocks and dryness, at last the ocean. But "Jody knew something was there, something very wonderful because it wasn't known, something secret and mysterious. He could feel within himself that this was so" (p. 241). That sense of the mysterious, the unknown, is unlocked by old Gitano. But when Jody presses Gitano for answers, Gitano simply refuses to tell him. The discovery of mystical transcendence, of a power that lies beyond human understanding, is finally one that each person makes individually.

The questing mind and the deep sensitivity to the transcendent dream admit Jody more fully than any other family member to Grandfather's vision of westering. To the others his tales are just old stories, repeated too often in the fashion of the elderly who have outlived their time and vaguely irritating because they divert attention from pragmatic realities. Grandfather has had his place in the sun, but the sun is declining on the wall of the Tiflin kitchen. Does it matter to Carl how he got this farm, when all of his concern is for its present demands? Does the dream of new possibilities have any influence over actions at this place, actions ruled by responsibilities rather than possibilities? For Carl the answer is adamantly no. But Jody's mind is of a different cast. He has sensed the vision of the transcendent power of a larger dream in old Gitano. Furthermore, he has witnessed the death of his beloved colt, but also the birth of a new colt from the death of Nellie. Intuitively, he has arrived at a deep sensitivity to new life arising from the passing of the old, but also the congruence of the old and new. This hunger for life is raw in him and is nurtured by Grandfather's vision of westering.

The westering concept has been the subject of considerable debate by Steinbeck scholars. Seen by some simply as an old man's maudlin and rambling recollection, it appears to be a flaw in the pattern of the tales. Seen by others as an adumbration of Steinbeck's phalanx theory—which it most certainly is—some have failed to see its close tie to the maturation of Jody and his growing vision of life and death.[20] Grandfather doesn't simply lament the loss of leadership; he laments the loss of the vision that he calls "westering." Life has been reduced to the routine; the dream has disappeared. But Jody has experienced the dream. The legacy of westering now lives in him. The passing of the dream from old hands to new is signified by Jody's serving Grandfather the lemonade. Jody relinquishes the mouse hunt, something he has looked forward to for days and something entirely self-serving, in order to cheer up Grandfather. His selfless compassion marks him, in Grandfather's own terms, as the leader of the people who served others before himself. Robert

Morsberger observes, "'Westering' may be dead in subdivisions" in today's world,[21] but Steinbeck demonstrates in *The Red Pony* that the dream does indeed live on, that it may be handed from one generation to the next. Jody's maturation in the stories is, finally, the inheritance of the great vision.

Jody's maturation into knowledge of life and death and his appropriation of Grandfather's great dream of westering do not absolve all conflict, however. It would be more precise to say that he now holds life and death in tension, rather than to say that he sees a transcendent vision of a life force that abnegates death. The latter might be said about Joseph Wayne of *To a God Unknown*, who even while dying feels the rejuvenative surge of rain upon him. The tension develops, possibly, not out of Steinbeck's mystical attraction evidenced in Joseph Wayne, but out of his practical experience of the illness of his mother.

That tension is supplied in several ways in the stories. Billy Buck, whom Jody reveres above all men, finding in him a wisdom born of experience that transcends his father's sternness, is at once a life-bringer and executioner. He must smash Nellie's skull before bringing forth the colt, an action that also tears Billy apart for, as he says, "I'm half horse myself, you see." At the end of "The Promise," Billy Buck bears the blood from Nellie like a wound on his own face. It is that wound that Jody remembers, and the look of despair on Billy's face.

The tension is also supplied in the juxtaposed symbols of the cypress tree and the watering pipe. Frequently Jody wanders between these two places, always feeling a cold dread of the cypress tree and a warm sympathy for the watering place. The two places develop symbolically throughout the stories in direct intensity and proportion to Jody's own understanding of the life-death tension.

In "The Gift" the two are matter-of-factly introduced as physical places on the farm. While drinking from the trough by the spring, Jody can glance downhill and see the cypress:

> He leaned over and drank close to the green mossy wood where the water tasted best. Then he turned and looked back on the ranch, on the low, whitewashed house girded with red geraniums, and on the long bunkhouse by the cypress tree where Billy Buck lived alone. Jody could see the great black kettle under the cypress tree. That was where the pigs were scalded. [p. 204]

The cypress, traditional symbol of death and a feature of cemeteries, is immediately associated with death and loss. Having looked upon it, Jody feels "an uncertainty in the air, a feeling of change and of loss and of the gain of new and unfamiliar things" (p. 205). As if in response to the tremulous sense of fear, two black buzzards glide past.

The tension between cypress and watering place is emphasized when Gabilan becomes ill and Jody begins to sense the symbolism of the juxtaposition: "He looked down at the house and at the old bunkhouse and at the dark cypress tree. The place was familiar, but curiously changed. It wasn't itself any more, but a frame for things that were happening" (p. 235). Weighty and thick, the cypress hunkers like a perpetual shadow on the landscape of the story. The pellucid waters of the spring charge along a line of greenery to the watering trough where the animals nourish themselves. The pigs snuffle at the trough; behind them hangs the singletree and the black tub for slaughter.

In "The Great Mountains," where Jody's sense of life and death broadens from the experience of Gabilan to human experiences in old Gitano, the cypress-watering place symbolism intensifies. Having just killed the thrush, Jody washes himself at the trough. It cleanses and rejuvenates, but the cypress stands unyieldingly before him.

In "The Promise" the symbolism is made overt, paralleling Jody's own growth in understanding the tensions of life and death:

> The water whined softly into the trough all the year round. This place had grown to be a center-point for Jody. When he had been punished the cool green grass and the singing water soothed him. When he had been mean the biting acid of meanness left him at the brush line. When he sat in the grass and listened to the purling stream, the barriers set up in his mind by the stern day went down to ruin. (pp. 268–69)

The trough is the "center-point," but the cypress is the counter-point:

> On the other hand, the black cypress tree by the bunkhouse was as repulsive as the water-tub was dear; for to this tree all the pigs came, sooner or later, to be slaughtered. Pig killing was fascinating, with the screaming and the blood, but it made Jody's heart beat so fast that it hurt him. After the pigs were scalded in the big iron tripod kettle and their skins were scraped and white, Jody had to go to the water-tub to sit in the grass until his heart grew quiet. The water-tub and the black cypress were opposites and enemies. [p. 269]

Immediately Jody associates the opposition with Nellie and the unborn colt, Black Demon. The trilling water nurtures his dream for the colt, but he cannot escape the presence of the cypress. As Jody walks into the barn when Nellie is due, he walks through a blackness in which only the cypress stands out, a darker blackness against the night.

Neither the tree nor the trough appears in "The Leader of the People." The symbolism is manifested in life itself with the appearance of Grandfather. This time, Billy Buck states the tension as Jody prepares to attack the mice in the haystack:

> Jody changed his course and moved toward the house. He leaned his flail against the steps. "That's to drive the mice out," he said. "I'll bet they're fat. I'll bet they don't know what's going to happen to them today."
>
> "No, nor you either," Billy remarked philosophically. "Nor me, nor anyone."
>
> Jody was staggered by this thought. He knew it was true. His imagination twitched away from the mouse hunt. (pp. 299–300)

Here the tension is stated overtly: Death and life hang in a delicate balance. This too has been Jody's discovery in the course of his maturation.

* * *

Lev Shestov, writing on the conflict between reason and revelation in his major work *Athens and Jerusalem*, argues that our present age is trapped in the cold hands of pragmatic necessity. His essential question might serve as a coda for *The Red Pony*:

> Is it given men to judge the truths, to decide the fate of the truths? On the contrary, it is the truths which judge men and decide their fate and not men who rule over the truths. Men, the great as well as the small, are born and die, appear and disappear—but the truth remains.[22]

Jody senses the truth in a way that Carl Tiflin will never approach. From the "little boy Jody," checked constantly by his father's discipline, dignity, and occasional cruelty, he has matured not necessarily to adult wisdom but to a sense of fullness of life that holds living and dying, reality and the dream, in balance. The passage has required loss and desolation, but it has produced the tempered steel of actions of the heart.

Against a backdrop of enervating personal turmoil, *The Red Pony* represents an artistic triumph for Steinbeck. The carefully paced theme of maturity through the desolation of loss, and the heightened sense of a transcendent vision that rises above the narrowness of pragmatic reality, carry the weight of a deeply meaningful work. The artistic craftsmanship, the carefully plotted patterns of description, symbolism, and imagery, carry the energy of an intriguing and moving story. It is an enduring work, a classic by virtue of its profound simplicity, unswervingly faithful in capturing the childhood point of view, disciplined in its narration.

Moreover, in the development of his fictional artistry, the sequence of stories represents a liberation for Steinbeck. In them he moves to the heart of his artistic talent. It is a historical irony that he completed *The Pastures of Heaven* and *The Red Pony* while simultaneously revising *To a God Unknown*, for these separate works represent the dialectic of his fictional career: stories of personal experience and a recollected past versus a story of philosophical breadth and open-ended speculation. Finding now some scant degree of commercial success with the former—as much as the whimsical wrath of the Great Depression would allow—Steinbeck felt a degree of benediction upon the kind of story he wanted to tell, the stories of *his* heart. A path opened for him in *The Red Pony* that would be well traveled in future years. Even in such a work as *In Dubious Battle*, to be undertaken in the year following and in which Steinbeck grapples with the concept of mob action, he located that concept surely and deliberately in the places and people he knew firsthand.

Notes

1. Benson, *True Adventures*, p. 262. In the ledger notebook Steinbeck entered a note that tied together his mother's illness and the theme of his stories. After observing the challenge "to know the sorrow in it and to feel it not in myself but in herself," he announces, "And that is the new theme. Curious that the greatest conceptions should come to me in this time of trouble. I wonder whether Carol can be right when she says it is because of the trouble. . . . Even a few lines written every night would make me feel better" (*LVN*).

2. "The Murder" and "The Chrysanthemums" were the first two stories written in the *Long Valley* collection. Both were completed and sent to George Albee for comment by February 25, 1934. Their probable dates of composition were December 1933 for "The Murder" and December–February 1934 for "The Chrysanthemums." On November 23, 1933, Steinbeck wrote of having finished the first draft of *Tortilla Flat* (*SLL*, pp. 89–90), dating the composition of that manuscript from August to November 1933. In the summer of 1934, Steinbeck returned to the *Tortilla Flat* manuscript with a clearer concept of thematic unity (*SLL*, pp. 96–97).

3. Joseph Fontenrose, *John Steinbeck: An Introduction and Interpretation*, p. 63.

4. Joseph Warren Beach, "John Steinbeck: Journeyman Artist," in *American Fiction: 1920–1940*, p. 314. Steinbeck was very much conscious of a similarity between *The Red Pony* and *The Yearling*. In February 1941 he wrote Elizabeth Otis regarding the film production of *The Red Pony*:

I wish you would read *The Yearling* again. Just a little boy named Jody has affection for a deer. Now I know there is no plagiarism on *The Red Pony*. But we are going to make *The Red Pony*, and two stories about a little boy in relation to animals is too much, particularly if in both cases the little boy's name is Jody. Will you see if we can't stop them from using the name and as much of the story as seems possible? If we don't want money we might easily get a court order. [*SLL*, p. 225]

Marjorie Rawlings began work on *The Yearling* in March 1936, over two years after "The Gift" had been published in the *North American Review*. Rawlings worked on the book for well over a year, at one point throwing out the manuscript altogether, finally restarting and completing it in December 1937. When it did appear in the spring of 1938, *The Yearling* became an immediate best seller, winning the Pulitzer Prize for that year. For details of Rawlings's composition, see A. Scott Berg, *Max Perkins: Editor of Genius* (New York: E. P. Dutton, 1978).

5. Arnold L. Goldsmith, "Thematic Rhythm in *The Red Pony*," *College English* 26 (Feb. 1965): 391–94.

6. Mimi R. Gladstein, "'The Leader of the People': A Boy Becomes a 'Mensch,'" in *Steinbeck's "The Red Pony": Essays in Criticism*, ed. Tetsumaro Hayashi and Thomas J. Moore, pp. 27–37.

7. R. Baird Shuman, "Initiation Rites in Steinbeck's *The Red Pony*," *English Journal* 59, no. 9 (Dec. 1970): 1252–55.

8. Frederic I. Carpenter, "John Steinbeck: American Dreamer," in *Steinbeck and His Critics: A Record of Twenty-Five Years*, ed. E. W. Tedlock, Jr., and C. V. Wicker, p. 77.

9. Lisca, *Wide World*, p. 10.

10. See Donald E. Houghton, "'Westering' in 'Leader of the People,'" *Western American Literature* 4 (Summer 1969): 117–24, and Robert E. Morsberger, "In Defense of 'Westering,'" *Western American Literature* 5 (Summer 1970): 143–46. Houghton argues that Grandfather's "explanation of westering is an unfortunate, confusing, and unnecessary digression which tears at the emotional and thematic unity of this story and of *The Red Pony* as a whole" (p. 124). Morsberger correctly takes some of the historical, critical, and philosophical errors of the essay to task.

11. Robert S. Hughes, Jr., "The Black Cypress and the Green Tub: Death and Procreation in Steinbeck's 'The Promise,'" in *Steinbeck's "The Red Pony": Essays in Criticism*, pp. 9–16.

12. French, "Introduction," in *Steinbeck's "The Red Pony*," p. xii.

13. Each of the *Red Pony* stories was published independently in periodicals. They first appeared together as a collection in a special issue by Covici-Friede in 1937, in which 699 copies were published and signed by Steinbeck, but the most convenient pagination occurs with their publication in *The Long Valley*. All page references in this study are to *The Long Valley*.

14. Goldsmith, "Thematic Rhythm," p. 392.

15. Ibid.

16. John Steinbeck, "My Short Novels," *Wings* 26 (Oct. 1953): 4.

17. In "Who Is 'The Leader of the People'?: Helping Students Examine Fiction," *English Journal* 48 (Nov. 1959), Alfred Grommen points out that Carl "is, ironically, unequal to the stature of his ten-year-old son and the old man" (p. 455).

Except that Jody is nearer age twelve in this story, it is true that Carl and Jody's behavioral rules are reversed in the final story.

18. As the mice-hunt episode develops in the ledger, the significance of the mice themselves undergoes an interesting change. In the first mention of it, Steinbeck wrote, "Those fat sleek arrogant mice were doomed." After commenting, "They had grown smug in their security, overbearing and fat. But the time of disaster had come," he links the mice to certain social orders. A passage that originally read, "The [undecipherable word] of mother mice, the carcasses of political mice, the gossiping clicks of social mice, the young fiery mice, all would go to the death" was revised simply to "They would not survive another day."

19. John Steinbeck, *East of Eden*, p. 3.

20. In "Something That Happened: A Non-Teleological Approach to 'The Leader of the People,'" *Steinbeck Quarterly* 6 (Winter 1973), Richard Astro claims that Jody's concern for Grandfather arises from "his juvenile fantasies of adventure which distinctly prohibit him from understanding the true meaning of Grandfather's expression of the unifying aspirations of the 'group man'" (p. 22). Thus, in Astro's view Jody's attraction is to the sense of adventure rather than to his Grandfather and his dream.

21. Morsberger, "In Defense of 'Westering,'" p. 146.

22. Lev Shestov, *Athens and Jerusalem*, trans. Bernard Martin, p. 76–77. Shestov argues that the apprehension of truth must be wrested from the grip of what he calls Necessity, the equivalent in Steinbeck's view of pragmatic reality, or civilization. Shestov comments, "Both men and gods must again learn it from the very Necessity which itself learns nothing, knows nothing, and wishes to know nothing, which is not concerned with any thing or any person and which despite this—without wishing or seeking it—has been reared so high above everything existing that gods and men all become equal before it, equal in rights or, more correctly, equal in the lack of all rights" (p. 126).

ROBERT M. BENTON

A Search for Meaning in "Flight"

It is quite unusual to find unanimity of opinion among literary critics, but in regard to "Flight" all seem to concur that it is one of Steinbeck's most finely crafted stories. Some believe it to be without peer. The power and artistry of "Flight" are obvious even on a first reading. Taken generally as a story of passage to maturity, it demonstrates no waste or unnecessary action, presenting the major narrative action in as direct a manner as possible.

Pepé Torres is sent by his widowed mother to Monterey for medicine and salt. Given his father's hat and riding on his father's saddle while boasting of his own manhood, Pepé goes to Monterey, drinks too much wine, gets into a fight, and kills a man. When he returns home, he tells his mother what happened and prepares to escape into the mountains. With his father's black coat, a bag of jerky, a rifle, and ten cartridges, Pepé travels into the mountains at night. After four days of increasing difficulty, he is killed by his pursuers. It is a simple story line with a clearly predictable outcome.

"Flight" might be seen as too finely crafted, too sparsely detailed, and too lightly motivated. When directors attempt to film such carefully crafted Steinbeck stories, the unfortunate result is often the encumbering of the story with details that remove all mystery and ruin Steinbeck's intended effect. This story is titled "Flight," and it is Pepé's flight upon which Steinbeck wants to focus the readers' attention.

From *Steinbeck's Short Stories in* The Long Valley: *Essays in Criticism*, edited by Tetsumaro Hayashi, pp. 18–25. Copyright © 1991 by Tetsumaro Hayashi.

Although this is a story of adolescence, of the boy becoming a man, Pepé does not achieve maturity until he begins his journey into the mountains. He is first described to the reader as one of the three Torres children, "the tall smiling son of nineteen, a gentle, affectionate boy, but very lazy . . . his mouth was as sweet and shapely as a girl's mouth, and his chin was fragile and chiseled. He was loose and gangling, all legs and feet and wrists, and he was very lazy."[1] Pepé seems totally preoccupied with his inheritance from his father, a switchblade knife with which he has become extremely adept.

Mama Torres ridicules Pepé's doing "foolish things with the knife, like a toy-baby," and she "took him by one loose shoulder and hoisted at him" (p. 28). When he leaves for Monterey, proclaiming "I am a man," his mother's retort is, "Thou art a foolish chicken" (p. 29). Once Pepé rides away, he is no longer seen by the reader. The focus remains on Mama Torres, who is asked by one of her younger children if Pepé has become a man by riding into Monterey. Her reply foreshadows the impending action: "A boy gets to be a man when a man is needed" (p. 30).

Steinbeck wisely omits all details of Pepé's trip to Monterey. Although this is a story of a boy's maturing, Pepé does not achieve that maturity in the bar when he kills a man. His rash, impetuous action is all adolescence, and it does not help to prejudice the reader by scenes that Steinbeck correctly wanted to leave to the reader's imagination. Had the confrontation in the Monterey bar been described by the omniscient narrator, readers would have been distracted by those events.

Pepé is allowed to tell his own story, the essence of which the narrator reports:

> A few people came into the kitchen of Mrs. Rodriguez. There was wine to drink. Pepé drank wine. The little quarrel—the man started toward Pepé and then the knife—it went almost by itself. It flew, it darted before Pepé knew it. As he talked, Mama's face grew stern, and it seemed to grow more lean. Pepé finished. "I am a man now, Mama. The man said names to me I could not allow." (p. 31)

The narration includes almost no details, and there is a sense of the knife's having a will of its own. Rather than being an extension of the boy, it acts and drags the boy along with it.

Pepé appears to believe that the experience in the Monterey bar transformed him into a man, and Mama Torres seems to agree with him. "Mama nodded. 'Yes, thou art a man, my poor little Pepé'" (p. 31). Even though she calls him her "poor little Pepé," Mama and many of the critics believe maturity comes with the killing. Steinbeck may have felt otherwise. Pepé's post-murder activity is still that of an adolescent. He runs. The story is, in fact, a flight, only a flight, and nothing if not a flight. He has yet to face the consequences of his actions.

In his construction of the early parts of the story, Steinbeck allows the reader to feel pity for Pepé: for the rashness of his adolescence, for the suffering he experiences in the mountains, and for his eventual death. Since the reader is not allowed a specific view of Pepé's rashness, pity can be focused on the flight alone.

Up to the time when Pepé leaves home for the mountains, the only strong character in the story is Mama Torres, whom Mimi R. Gladstein calls "the best example of an indestructible woman in a short story."[2] Mama Torres is credited with having the "traditional patience of woman" in her tolerance of "Pepé's childish preoccupation with his knife," a tolerance mixed with scorn for such aggressive action.

Mimi R. Gladstein believes that Pepé's "aggressive masculine behavior leads to Pepé's killing a man. A man challenges him and he responds with a phallic symbol, the knife."[3] She also asserts that "Pepé's aggression and knife-throwing identify him with manhood," but his aggression must remain an interpretation not borne out in the account except by implication. Aggressive behavior can just as easily be called adolescent behavior as masculine. Gladstein also attributes to Mama Torres the characteristics of giving, nourishing behavior and endurance through pain. Such a suggestion, then, allows Gladstein to suggest that it is Steinbeck the sentimentalist who "edges out" Steinbeck the scientist.

The above interpretation does not account for significant aspects of Mama Torres's behavior and actions that tend to change the focus of "Flight" and create the emphasis Steinbeck the scientist seems everywhere to maintain. What is to be made of Mama's taunting of Pepé before sending him to Monterey? She compares him to a lazy cow, calls him a toy-baby for the foolish things he does with his knife, and, when she tells him he is to go for the medicine, calls him "Big Lazy" and "Peanut." Pepé proclaims that he is a man, but Mama again calls him a peanut, and when he is on the horse and ready to leave, she says he is a "foolish chicken." Are these the characteristics of giving, nourishing behavior or of a tired, realistic observer of her own issue?

It does seem clear that Steinbeck is asking the reader to consider when the boy becomes a man, but he may be asking that readers evaluate Pepé's contentions, Mama's evaluation, and the boy's actions in order to arrive at a clear understanding of when Pepé does achieve real maturity. If that is true, Steinbeck, like Faulkner, requires the reader to become a participant in determining the truth of the matter. Forced to deal with the consequences of his adolescent action, Pepé struggles to understand what this means to him.

Richard Astro gives a valid assessment when he says, "It is in his moment of crisis, Steinbeck seems to say, that a boy must break through to manhood."[4] The problem for the reader, however, is to determine when that moment of crisis occurs. The structure of the narrative suggests that breaking through has not yet happened when Pepé leaves home a second time and heads into the mountains.

Too many problems become apparent if one assumes that Pepé achieves manhood when he kills. Such an interpretation would suggest that the climax of the story, the moment when the adolescent achieves maturity, is never presented to the reader except through the narrator's paraphrase of Pepé's confession to Mama Torres. Those who wish to pursue such a belief are forced to see the story in ways that Steinbeck seemed determined to avoid.

In his analysis of the Barnaby Conrad and Louis Bisbo feature-length film of "Flight," Joseph R. Millichap summarizes the murder scene: "In adolescent self-assertion, he accidentally kills a man in a drunken brawl. The dead man's friends then pursue him into the mountains and kill him."[5] The only information Steinbeck gives in the story is, "There was wine to drink. Pepé drank wine. The little quarrel—the man started toward Pepé and then the knife—it went almost by itself" (p. 31).

The information Steinbeck reveals, if, in fact, it is even intended to be seen as accurate, does not allow the interpretation that this is a scene of a drunken brawl. The material Steinbeck relates is as sparse as could be imagined. Furthermore, even though a reader might assume that the friends of the murdered man formed a posse to hunt down Pepé, the story does not sanction such emendation. Millichap does acknowledge that the original film padded the story and added long sections that were not in the original, including a cafe brawl, but he gives this information only after he describes the murder on the basis of such a brawl. How easy it is to allow one's personal conceptions to become entangled with an author's presentation, and how misleading such an interpretation can be!

The clearest indication of Steinbeck's emphasis is first related in the description of Pepé when he returns from Monterey:

> He was changed. The fragile quality seemed to have gone from his chin. His mouth was less full than it had been, the lines of the lips were straighter, but in his eyes the greatest change had taken place. There was no laughter in them any more, nor any bashfulness. They were sharp and bright and purposeful. (p. 31)

Undoubtedly, the reader is forced to see that this is a different Pepé from the one who left boasting of his manhood. Although he concludes his account of the murder with another affirmation of his manhood, Mama is not fully able to accept his maturity.

When he returns from Monterey, Pepé is changed, but it is only through his flight that he will come to accept his full responsibility and become a man. Mama Torres still has to tell him how to travel, when to stop, and how to eat. She also warns him, "When thou comest to the high mountains, if thou seest any of the dark watching men, go not near to them nor try to speak to them" (p. 33). Once he leaves and has become "a grey, indefinite shadow" (p. 33), she gives him up. She relaxes and begins the death wail.

Pepé follows Mama's instructions well: he cares for his horse, walking it when possible and letting it drink from the stream running out the canyon; he does not look back, and he drinks and eats sparingly. Once in the canyon, he is in a beautiful, fertile world. Steinbeck describes the "perfumed and purple light" and the gooseeberry and blackberry bushes lining the stream.

Steinbeck extends the pastoral quality of the scene by noting the splashing waterfalls and how the "five-fingered ferns hung over the water and dripped spray from their fingertips" (p. 35). Pepé is distracted by the scene with one leg "dangling" loose as he picks a bay leaf, but sounds of an approaching rider call him back to reality. He hides behind a tree and, once the horseman is past, he no longer relaxes. Placing a cartridge in the rifle, Pepé prepares himself to enter a new world where "the redwood trees were smaller and their tops were *dead*, bitten *dead* where the wind reached them" (p. 35) (emphasis mine).

Pepé now moves cautiously, accompanied by a host of death symbols. Louis Owens describes Pepé's flight as "both away from death and toward death; it is Everyman's flight."[6] Owens extensively notes the symbols of death that Steinbeck uses in the creation of a "psychic waste land." Pepé quickly looks away from his glimpse of a black figure he knows as one of the dark watchers, but the blackness becomes an increasing presence. No sooner has Pepé passed over one mountain than he is confronted with another, "desolate with dead rocks and starving little black bushes" (p. 37).

Steinbeck's inclusion of the images of the "dark watchers" continues to puzzle readers. An entire spectrum of interpretations has been attempted, but few give helpful insights. John Antico believes that they "symbolize the death that is in store for Pepé," appearing as "premonitions of what is to come."[7] A similar view is held by John Ditsky: "The dark watchers are, I suggest, the walking dead of folk myth, whose company Pepé at last joins."[8] Louis Owens suggests that "the dark watchers are 'dream symbols' rising up to sight from the low dark levels of man's awareness of the death that stand in Steinbeck's fiction as symbols of death and the unknown."[9]

No definitive explanation of the dark watchers seems possible, nor need one be sought. When Pepé first left for Monterey, Mama warned against improper devotion in the church: "You would sit there flapping your mouth over Aves all day while you looked at the candles and the holy pictures" (p. 29). Her later caution about the dark watchers suggests that a combination of religion, folk myth, and superstition ruled daily activities. Since the dark watchers "watch," but do not act, they are apt symbols for a naturalistic work. They deepen the resonance of the story and heighten the symbolic significance without providing specific meaning. To call them "symbols of death and the unknown," as Owens does, will provide as much insight as one is likely to find.

Other symbols seem much more clear and more in keeping with the focus Steinbeck provides in Pepé's flight. In a moment of rest while letting his horse graze, Pepé takes a string of jerky and moves under an oak. "He sat down in the crisp dry oak leaves and automatically felt for his big black knife to cut the jerky, but he had no knife" (p. 38). He had left the knife in the stranger he killed in Monterey. After a short sleep, he awakens at the sound of horse hooves on the rock and quickly resumes his flight, forgetting his hat under the tree.

Struggling until the first light of dawn, Pepé again stops to look back, drink water, and eat jerky. Before he hears the sound of the rifle, his horse drops and dies. Now Pepé "moved with the instinctive care of an animal" (p. 40). Creeping behind a rock and studying movements in the chaparral below, Pepé shoots toward the brush. Another shot from below grazes the rock, and the sheared granite lodges in his hand. Wriggling toward the ridge peak, Pepé comes close to a rattlesnake, and later, when a lizard pauses in front of him, he crushes it with a stone.

Exhausted and desperate with wounded hand and swollen tongue, Pepé discards his coat. Later he tries to suck water from a handful of mud, only to suffer worse results from the poultice-like clay. He sleeps when the heat of the day beats down on him, only to awaken with a mountain lion staring at him from twenty feet. Still his pursuers come. Darkness falls again, and Pepé works his way on up the hill, forgetting his rifle and unable to discover where he had left it.

Once he has discarded or lost all trappings of civilization—knife, hat, coat, and rifle—he becomes more completely animal-like. He moves with the "effort of a hurt beast," and when he tries to make words "only a thick hissing came from between his lips" (p. 44). His swollen arm reveals gangrene from wrist to armpit, but without his knife he can only use a sharp rock to scrape at the wound, sawing at the flesh until he can squeeze out the infection. "Instantly he threw back his head and whined like a dog" (p. 44). Until this moment, he has struggled to survive, but when he looks skyward and sees vultures soaring overhead, he accepts the verdict of nature.

Pepé's flight toward death is fully orchestrated by Steinbeck. The farther into the mountains Pepé moves, the more frequent are the natural images of desolation. The fertile canyons with waterfalls and foliage are replaced with trees described as "smaller and their tops were dead, bitten dead where the wind reached them" (p. 35). Pepé leaves the stream and "the soft black earth" to meet mountains "desolate with dead rocks and starving little black bushes" (p. 37). Ahead he sees "the sharp snaggled edge of the ridge . . . , rotten granite tortured and eaten by the winds of time" (p. 39).

As Pepé's condition becomes more desperate, he faces "the jagged rotten teeth of the mountain" (p. 42), the "granite teeth" poised at the dawn of his last day. Finally, he prepares himself for the final judgment. Quickly bowing his head and crossing himself, Pepé struggles to the top of a large rock on the ridge peak where he stands "erect" to accept the execution his juvenile rashness made inevitable.

When Pepé is struck by bullets from the pursuers' guns, he topples forward, his rolling starting a small avalanche. "And when he at last stopped against a bush, the avalanche slid slowly down and covered up his head" (p. 46). This seems an appropriate conclusion to his short experience of being a man, but some believe that this final image suggests a deeper meaning that Steinbeck wants to imply. It is always tempting to search for a clue that will provide startling insight.

Chester Chapin suggests that Pepé is "a boy of subnormal intelligence, a mental defective."[10] Chapin is then led to assert that Pepé had a deformed head that Steinbeck allows nature, in Pepé's death, to "mercifully" conceal. Chapin compares Pepé with Lennie of *Of Mice and Men* and justifies Pepé's death on the basis of his inability to cope with life. This is, indeed, a startling interpretation, but it is so devoid of support in the narrative that it strains the wildest imagination.

"Flight" is a story dramatizing the passage from adolescence to maturity. It does show how Pepé becomes a man, but that passage takes place during the flight. Nothing in the story implies that Pepé returns from Monterey a man, and Steinbeck's omission of the scene in the bar, except through Pepé's recounting it to his mother, is sufficient evidence that the single focus of the story is the flight itself. In that flight into the mountains, Pepé gains insight into the grave consequences that his rash, adolescent act brings. When he can acknowledge that he is responsible for his actions, he then stands erect and presents himself for judgment, demonstrating that he has achieved manhood. Rather than being a mental defective unable to cope with life, Pepé reveals himself as one who has come to realize what nature requires of a man who accepts responsibility for his own acts. His death may be cruel, but it is in keeping with the mores of his society. He finally has achieved the kind of dignity that is bestowed on one who accepts himself and the consequences of his behavior.

Notes

1. John Steinbeck, "Flight" in *The Long Valley* (New York: Bantam Books, 1967), pp. 26–27. Subsequent quotations from "Flight" will be noted by page number in parentheses following the quotation.

2. Mimi Reisel Gladstein, "Female Characters in Steinbeck: Minor Characters of Major Importance?" *Steinbeck's Women: Essays in Criticism*, ed. Tetsumaro Hayashi (*Steinbeck Monograph Series*, No. 9) (Muncie, Indiana: Steinbeck Society, Ball State University, 1979), p. 22.

3. *Ibid*.

4. Richard Astro, *John Steinbeck and Edward F. Ricketts: The Shaping of a Novelist* (Minneapolis: University of Minnesota Press, 1973), p. 115.

5. Joseph R. Millichap, *Steinbeck and Film* (New York: Frederick Ungar Publishing Company, 1983), p. 162.

6. Louis Owens, *John Steinbeck's Re-Vision of America* (Athens: University of Georgia Press, 1985), p. 30.

7. John Antico, "A Reading of Steinbeck's 'Flight,'" *Modern Fiction Studies*, 11 (Spring 1965), 48.

8. John Ditsky, "Steinbeck's 'Flight': The Ambiguity of Manhood," *Steinbeck Quarterly*, 5 (Summer–Fall 1973), 83.

9. Owens, p. 32.

10. Chester F. Chapin, "Pepé Torres: A Steinbeck 'Natural,'" *College English*, 23 (May 1962), 676.

SUSAN SHILLINGLAW

"*The Chrysanthemums*": *Steinbeck's* Pygmalion

For John Steinbeck "life was not a struggle toward anything, but a constant process in it," writes Jackson J. Benson, and "that process for man . . . was largely a matter of learning. It was the major 'action' for both his life and work."[1] It is clearly the major "action" in his two most famous stories about women, "The Chrysanthemums" and "The White Quail." As Steinbeck records in his journals, the germ for each is that moment when a woman learns something profound about herself, a moment of insight either grasped or denied: Elisa seeing the chrysanthemums on the road; Mary in her garden, looking in the window. Before he composed "The Chrysanthemums" in 1934, Steinbeck wrote:

> I wish I could get the lady and the chrysanthemums out of my mind. If she goes much further, I'll have to write her and I haven't the least idea what she's about. I'm afraid she's going to get me and she isn't much of a story any way. But she is interesting and if she did see them along side the road—what the hell. She'd feel pretty terrible if she had built up a structure. And if her structure were built on an inner joy, all the more.[2]

Clearly what intrigues Steinbeck is the instant when the structure, her envisioned life, topples completely. Such crises often appear in Steinbeck's

From *Steinbeck's Short Stories in* The Long Valley: *Essays in Criticism*, edited by Tetsumaro Hayashi, pp. 1–9. Copyright © 1991 by Tetsumaro Hayashi.

work—although many of his characters certainly resist knowledge. But not Elisa. Hers is a story about change.

I would like to suggest a source for this tale about Elisa Allen's knowledge—the Pygmalion legend. For an author whose works frequently draw upon a mythic tradition, it is hardly surprising that this story of metamorphosis reveals his debts to both Ovid and George Bernard Shaw in delineating the stifling effects of both sexual repression and middle-class complacency.

In Ovid's version, the motive for transformation is sexual. Disgusted with the Propoetides, the whorish women he knows, the artist Pygmalion imagines an ideal woman, carves her in stone, and lovingly caresses her. And Venus, rewarding him for envisioning this ideal, grants Pygmalion the wish he dares not utter, the transformation of his statue into a woman. In Shaw's version of the legend, however, the sexual energy is diffused; Henry Higgins's sublime female is his mother, not the fair Eliza. Urging Eliza to stay with him at the end of the play, he offers her only a cozy triangle of her, Higgins, and Pickering, "three bachelors." He defines a complete life thus: "I care for life, for humanity, and you are a part of it that has come my way and been built into my house. What more can you or anyone ask?"[3] For him, Eliza Doolittle exists as an object, a useful piece of furniture. Triumphantly, he brags of the transformation she desires and he effects—not asexual change but a social one, a change of class. Yet the metamorphosis does not free her. "Until the last scene of the play," notes one commentator, "Eliza is in a position of economic, as well as emotional and intellectual dependence on Higgins. She is a kept woman."[4] Pygmalion/Henry's dominance effects one metamorphosis, one that is, in effect, static, the creation of an articulate and finely dressed lady. But Lady Eliza must effect a second metamorphosis, specifically that from a kept woman to a free one. She must define life on her own terms. Thus, while making class the central issue, Shaw's play also studies the inadequacies of Pygmalion/Henry's intellectual ideal. The creative mind in both the classical and the nineteenth-century versions envisions an ideal woman who must live in order to respond. In Ovid, life rewards the creator; in Shaw, life reveals the inadequacies of the creator.

Steinbeck fuses the different emphases found in Ovid and Shaw. He shows the sexual repressions a woman feels, not just in a broad social sense, but in the sense that class differences imply various degrees of empowerment and repression.[5] He has taken Ovid and Shaw and made their myths his own representation of men and women in a bourgeois world they uncritically accept as the only one imaginable, despite the possibilities for revolution held out, albeit deceptively, by the tinker. The open road is really a dead end for Elisa.

In the beginning of the story Steinbeck's Elisa, like Shaw's Eliza, is a kept woman. The opening paragraphs that describe the valley suggest her

isolation, and, as Louis Owens notes, her "suspended life, awaiting the fertilizing imagination of the tinker."[6] But the figurative language also conveys
a sense of mechanized, transformed nature, and this, too, helps characterize
Elisa. Fog sits like a lid; the Salinas Valley is a closed pot; earth gleams like
metal; willow shrubs "flame with sharp and positive leaves,"[7] as if etched.
Nature, now held in check, has undergone a metamorphosis into something
static and vaguely forbidding. And Elisa, the woman closest to nature, is similarly checked—fenced in when we first see her. In one of the best analyses of
the story, Marilyn Mitchell argues that both Eliza and Mary Teller of "The
White Quail" are "trapped between society's definition of the masculine and
the feminine and are struggling against the limitations of the feminine."[8]
More pointedly, it is the middle class—with all of the sexual, spiritual, and
social inhibitions it enforces—that traps Elisa, as it does many throughout
Steinbeck's work. She has been repressed by the very things which, while gardening, she achieves physical distance from—the tidy house behind her and
the men conversing "down" to her. But no psychological escape follows. The
syntax of the first sentence describing Elisa conveys her awareness of male
prerogatives: "Elisa Allen, working in her flower garden, looked down across
the yard and saw Henry, her husband, talking to two men in business suits"
(*LV*, p. 4). The main clause addresses her awareness of the empowered male,
but the phrase suggests her avocation. In the second page of the story that
describes her gardening activities, there are four references to Elisa's glances
toward this authoritative group, each of whom stands "with one foot on the
side of the little Fordson" tractor. Steinbeck repeatedly shows that the bourgeois world restricts Elisa's self definition and creativity. When first described,
she wears male clothing like a shield: "Her figure looked blocked and heavy
in her gardening costume, a man's black hat pulled low down over her eyes,
clodhopper shoes, a figured spring dress almost completely covered by a big
corduroy apron with four big pockets. . . . She wore heavy leather gloves to
protect her hands while she worked" (*LV*, p. 4). The male attire compromises
Elisa's sexual identity, and this blurred identity causes much of her frustration. The softness that she later so poignantly reveals is, initially, concealed
beneath the unwieldy clothing. Unconsciously, she "pulls on the gardening
glove again" when Henry approaches, not only steeling herself against him,
but revealing the impossibility at this point of identifying herself outside a
male sphere. Furthermore, nothing in Elisa's world gives her pure pleasure.
Even her creative outlet, gardening, is an adulterated delight: "The chrysanthemum stems seemed too small and easy for her energy" (*LV*, p. 10). When
Henry first speaks to her, he taints their beauty by applying the language of
commerce to the flowers, noting their size and wishing that she'd "work out
in the orchard and raise some apples that big" (*LV*, p. 5). Henry speaks the

language of power, particularly when compared to the tinker's later poetic rendering of a chrysanthemum as "a quick puff of colored smoke" (*LV*, p. 10). The paragraph that precedes the arrival of the tinker further reveals the psychological limitations of Elisa's gardening:

> With her trowel she turned the soil over and over, and smoothed it and patted it firm. Then she dug ten parallel trenches to receive the sets. Back at the chrysanthemum bed she pulled out the little crisp shoots, trimmed off the leaves of each one with her scissors and laid it on a small orderly pile. (*LV*, p. 6)

Her garden is as ordered and controlled as she is. The outlet she chooses is an inadequate substitute for the more fulfilling life that she, at this point, barely recognizes that she subconsciously craves.

For this earthy Elisa, like her Shavian predecessor, accepts the place that Henry/Pygmalion assigns her in his world, although chafing at its boundaries that limit physical, psychological, and sexual freedom. Throughout, it is the conversation between the two that best reflects the conventional nature of their partnership, the degree to which the metamorphosis that a husband effects is complete. Here, I would suggest that Steinbeck deliberately parodies the profession of Shaw's Henry Higgins, the grammarian. Although this Henry is a man of plain words, when Elisa is with him, his speech patterns hers. She speaks as plainly as he, often echoing his words. Coming toward her after completing his business deal, he first notes her "strong" crop, and she replies that "They'll be strong this coming year" (*LV*, p. 5). Henry then observes that she has a "gift with things" and Elisa agrees that she has "a gift with things, all right." When the conversation shifts from flowers, her responses become rote. To Henry's news and his proposal that they go to town, she repeatedly notes that his actions and suggestions are "good," a word to which she returns at the end of the story when she once again accepts her lot as the dutiful wife:

> She said loudly, to be heard above the motor, "It will be good, tonight, a good dinner." "Now you've changed again," Henry complained. He took one hand from the wheel and patted her knee. "I ought to take you in to dinner oftener. It would be good for both of us. We get so heavy out on the ranch." (*LV*, p. 17)

The blandness of "good" or "nice" reflects the sterility of their marriage. The word "heavy," earlier used to describe Elisa's male clothing, here suggests the oppression that she, in particular, feels on the ranch. And "strong," the other word that so frequently identifies Elisa or her activities, ironically underlines her powerlessness, in spite of her undoubted vitality. The few words that Henry knows, that Elisa echoes, and that the author uses to characterize both, identify not only the constrictions on their marriage, but more broadly the limitations of the bourgeois world.

In sharp contrast to this tight and tidy sphere, the tinker's entourage lacks order: "Up this road came a curious vehicle, curiously drawn" with squeaking wheels, a "crazy, loose-jointed wagon. . . . It was drawn by an old bay horse and a little grey-and-white burro," a mismatched team. "Words were painted on the canvas, in clumsy, crooked letters," some misspelled; paint drips beneath each letter (*LV*, p. 7). The wagon itself, compared to a prairie schooner, suggests a world far different from Elisa's—the myth of the West, of freedom, of enterprising souls, of self-sufficiency. Critics have suggested various reasons for her attraction to the tinker. In him, argues Marilyn L. Mitchell, she "finds a man whose strength seems to match hers" (Mitchell, p. 312). She responds, notes William V. Miller, to the romanticism of his "vagabond life"[9] and to her "desire for the freedom of the male," Richard F. Peterson maintains.[10] Without discounting any of these suggestions, I would argue that she responds first not to his mode of life but to the man himself, a man from a class different from her own. Unlike her husband, he is a laborer, as the emphasis in Steinbeck's description of him makes vividly clear: his suit is "worn" and "spotted with grease," his hat battered; his eyes "were full of the brooding that gets in the eyes of teamsters and of sailors"; and his "calloused hands" are "cracked, and every crack was a black line" (*LV*, p. 8). This big, disheveled itinerant works with his hands (an important focus throughout the story), as her bourgeois husband seemingly does not.

It is of less importance, I think, that this craftsman is false than that Elisa does not notice or care that he manipulates her. Both the tinker and Johnny Bear, observes Miller, embody "Steinbeck's ambiguous vision of the artist's morality," although "the tinker's manipulative art is conscious" (Miller, p. 71). This con artist immediately transforms Elisa, just as Steinbeck intended his own tale to have a startling impact on readers. This story, he wrote, "is designed to strike without the reader's knowledge. I mean he reads it casually and after it is finished feels that something profound has happened to him although he does not know what nor how."[11] Similarly, this rough-hewn Pygmalion causes something profound to occur; a dark Lawrentian man, as Peterson notes, he is the catalyst for Elisa's metamorphosis into a sexual, fulfilled woman.[12] With Henry she is cautious, stiff, and careful. With the tinker she expands immediately, laughing with him on his arrival. Then she stands up, takes off her gloves, and, when he mentions her flowers, she "melts," and her actions become eager and excited. Her language flows freely; gone are the staccato responses of her dialogue with Henry. Only when he uses the language of commerce, a speech all too familiar to her, does she resist him. But unlike Henry, he speaks both a commercial and a poetic language, and to the latter she responds, most particularly when he mentions her flowers. Elisa changes rapidly as she prepares her sprouts for the tinker to take, her gift to him of herself. Without discounting Mordecai Marcus's argument that the flowers represent her maternal urges, I would suggest that these "big," "strong" chrysanthemums more forcefully represent Elisa herself, just as the white quail represents Mary Teller.[13] So when the tinker seems to understand her soul—as Harry Teller cannot comprehend Mary's—Elisa imparts to him its meaning, the feeling expressed in her "planter's hands." Unlike her terse comments to Henry about these hands, Elisa's comments to the tinker are expansive. "I don't know how to tell you," she begins (*LV*, p. 11). Although Steinbeck again focuses on the potential inadequacy of language, in Elisa's longest, most impassioned speech, she finds words to express what Edward F. Ricketts called the experience of "breaking through," from contact with the earth to knowledge of the stars. It is an Emersonian moment of transcending the physical to the spiritual, what Steinbeck envisioned as "a section of great ecstasy" when he was still struggling to write the opening paragraphs.[14] And the climax, as most commentators have noted, is overtly sexual. To complete the metamorphosis from somebody's woman to her own, she must find both spiritual and physical fulfillment. From the tinker she needs only the briefest encouragement, for the moment is truly her own, and the change effected in her is complete, if, as all such heightened awareness must be, it is also transitory.

The rest of the story tells of Elisa's gradual withdrawal from this moment. In *The Long Valley* there are at least five stories about female sexuality, "The Chrysanthemums," "The White Quail," "The Snake," "The Murder," "Johnny Bear," and possibly more, and each is patterned like a sexual encounter—expositions, a climax where the language is rather explicitly sexual, and the aftermath. After her own orgasmic moment, Elisa engages herself once again with her physical reality, first by reaching for another, the tinker, to share awareness: "her hesitant fingers almost touched the cloth. Then her hand dropped to the ground. She crouched low like a fawning dog" (*LV*, p. 12). When she reaches for his leg, she reaches out her "planter's hands" to connect with human life, and retreats. She is "like a fawning dog" because the spiritualized moment known only to humans is gone, and she must return to the physical world, to a man whose real concerns are not with her feelings but with a meal on the table and a pot to mend.[15] Her brave assertions about female capabilities—so similar to the speeches of Shaw's Eliza at the end of the play—and her dreamy farewell to the tinker once again identify precisely what her bourgeois existence lacks—ecstasy:

"That's a bright direction. There's a glowing there." The sound of her whisper startled her. She shook herself free and looked about to see whether anyone had been listening. Only the dogs had heard. (*LV*, p. 14)

Once again, the dogs suggest her retreat to a world without visions, where she seeks physical compensations. The tinker's road is one she travels only in a car with her husband.

Unlike Shaw's flower girl, who is changed first to a lady, then to an independent woman, Steinbeck's Elisa, however "strong," cannot define herself in either sphere of male empowerment. A Shavian woman who has declared her independence is often unmarried, like Eliza, so can assert and act upon her sexual, economic, and social freedom. Elisa Allen, however, is trapped by the institution of marriage, the bulwark of middle class values. Whereas her predecessor exits triumphantly, Elisa shrinks in defeat. But she does not forgo her "strength" easily. After the tinker departs, she tries to transfer her heightened awareness into the physical pleasures that are hers also in her garden—vigorously scrubbing in the bath, carefully assessing her body, slowly dressing for dinner. But once again, the male presence begins to sap her strength, her sense of herself. She must "set herself for Henry's arrival," and, delaying his approach, sit "primly and stiffly down." Just as Elisa changes gradually back to her accustomed self, so, too, does the story return to the language and imagery of the first pages. As she awaits Henry, she "looked toward the river road where the willow-line was still yellow with frosted leaves so that under the high grey fog they seemed a thin band of sunshine. This was the only color in the grey afternoon. She sat unmoving for a long time. Her eyes blinked rarely" (*LV*, p. 15). Readjusting herself to her static world, Elisa is as unmoving as a statue—Henry/Pygmalion's creation once again. As a wife, she looks with clarity at the fog and the light that so poignantly suggest, as Miller argues, her feelings of entrapment and squelched hopes (Miller, pp. 69–70).

The end of the story reinforces her sense of failure. But readers are often unsettled and puzzled about Elisa's final retreat. Why does she ask about the fights? A glance at the original text may help answer that question. In an article entitled "The Text of Steinbeck's 'The Chrysanthemums,'" William R. Osborne discusses the differences between the text Steinbeck first published in *Harper's Magazine* in 1937 and the one included in his collection of stories, *The Long Valley*, in 1938.[16] One of the most substantive changes is in the paragraphs about Elisa's reaction to the "dark speck," her flowers thrown on the road. The original text ends with these sentences:

> She felt ashamed of her strong planter's hands that were no use,
> lying palms up in her lap. In a moment they had left behind them
> the man who had not known or needed to know what she said, the
> bargainer. She did not look back. (Osborne, p. 481)

Obviously more expository than the later version, this passage also returns
the reader more insistently to her earlier transcendent moment with references to her hands, her explanation, and her shame. Through these verbal
echoes, Steinbeck emphasizes the finality of her retreat from fulfillment.
Furthermore, the reference to her hands gives us a clue, I believe, to the
resolution of the story. Touch is Elisa's most acute sense, and she is attracted
to the hands of a different class—to the tinker's calloused and skillful
hands, to the "fighting gloves [that] get heavy and soggy with blood" (*LV*,
p. 17). These males from a class lower than her own seem in contact with
life, movement, freedom, and violence. As in Shaw's *Pygmalion*, Steinbeck
contrasts the enervating effects of one class with the freedom and energy
possible to the lower class. It thus seems wrong to argue that Elisa queries
Henry about the fights because she wishes to punish men. Elisa does not
hate men, but is fascinated by their power, the kind denied her. "Do Any
women ever go to the fights?" she asks her husband. "Some," but not many,
and certainly not the wife Elisa who knows that she is once again inside her
fence, or, at this point, inside Henry's car. Wine suffices because it must,
and Elisa cries weakly—"like an old woman"—because she accepts her fate.
She will never take the road again.

Steinbeck's treatment of the Pygmalion legend is thus much bleaker
than either Ovid's or Shaw's, both of which, however different, end in self-
assertion. As she exits, Elisa Allen cries not because she is yet weak or old,
but because she is defeated by the bourgeois vision she must accept as her
own. Ironically, the water that the land and the farmers so eagerly await at
the beginning of the story arrives at last: tears of death, however, not of life.

NOTES

1. Jackson J. Benson, *The True Adventures of John Steinbeck, Writer* (New York:
Viking Press, 1984), pp. 250–51.

2. John Steinbeck, unpublished ledger book, Steinbeck Research Center, San
Jose State University, p. 29.

3. George Bernard Shaw, *Pygmalion* (New York: Simon and Schuster, 1912),
p. 95.

4. A. M. Gibbs, "The End of *Pygmalion*," *The Art and Mind of Shaw: Essays
in Criticism* (New York: St. Martin's Press, 1983), p. 170.

5. Critics have been divided on precisely what oppresses and frustrates Elisa.
Peter Lisca, among others, suggests that her role as a woman is the source of her
unhappiness. Mordecai Marcus disagrees, quoting F. W. Watt's observation that

Elisa's desires are "ambiguously sexual and spiritual" and arguing that this "ambiguity combined with Elisa's pervasive combination of femininity and masculinity" is central to the story (p. 54). It does not seem to me that the two are mutually exclusive, and I wish to give the broadest possible definition for her unhappiness as a woman in a culture that frustrates many desires.

6. Louis D. Owens, *John Steinbeck's Re-Vision of America* (Athens: University of Georgia Press, 1985), p. 109.

7. John Steinbeck, "The Chrysanthemums," *The Long Valley* (New York: Viking Press, 1938), p. 3. Subsequent citations from this work will appear as *LV.*

8. Marilyn L. Mitchell, "Steinbeck's Strong Women: Feminine Identity in the Short Stories," *Southwest Review*, 61 (Summer 1976), 306.

9. William V. Miller, "Sexual and Spiritual Ambiguity in 'The Chrysanthemums,'" *Steinbeck Quarterly*, 5 (Summer–Fall 1972), 71.

10. Richard F. Peterson, "The God in the Darkness: A Study of John Steinbeck and D. H. Lawrence," *Steinbeck's Literary Dimension: A Guide to Comparative Studies*, ed. Tetsumaro Hayashi (Metuchen, New Jersey: Scarecrow Press, 1973), p. 69.

11. Elaine Steinbeck and Robert Wallsten, eds., *Steinbeck: A Life in Letters* (New York: Viking Press, 1975), p. 91.

12. Both Richard F. Peterson and Roy S. Simmonds note the similarities between Steinbeck and Lawrence; Simmonds observes that the tinker is a "romantically virile man of nature who (only symbolically in this story, however) seduces her." I would add emphasis to this point by noting that class differences here, as in Lawrence, contribute to the attraction. "The Original Manuscripts of Steinbeck's 'The Chrysanthemums,'" *Steinbeck Quarterly*, 7 (Summer–Fall 1974), 107.

13. Mordecai Marcus, "The Lost Dream of Sex and Childbirth in 'The Chrysanthemums,'" *Modern Fiction Studies*, 11 (Spring 1965), 54–58.

14. Simmonds, 104. It seems fairly certain that Steinbeck is referring to this section of the story; he envisioned both his scene and the one where Elisa sees the chrysanthemums on the road, as discussed above, before he wrote the story, showing how significant that moment of change or insight is to his conception of the tale.

15. In a recent article, C. Kenneth Pellow argues that Elisa is "like a fawning dog" because she retires, as do the tinker's dogs, "from a potential fight, the struggle to free herself from a situation in which she feels trapped" (p. 10). His interpretation of this moment is close to my own. "'The Chrysanthemums' Revisited," *Steinbeck Quarterly*, 22 (Winter–Spring 1989), 8–16.

16. William R. Osborne, "The Texts of Steinbeck's 'The Chrysanthemums,'" *Modern Fiction Studies*, 12 (Winter 1966–67), 470–84.

CHRISTOPHER S. BUSCH

Longing for the Lost Frontier: Steinbeck's Vision of Cultural Decline in "The White Quail" and "The Chrysanthemums"

In the course of his forty-year career, John Steinbeck consistently integrated elements of American frontier history, mythology, and symbolism into his fiction and nonfiction. Steinbeck's fascination with the frontier past germinated during his boyhood in Salinas, at that time a cowtown described by Jackson J. Benson as "a throwback to the frontier towns of a half-century before."[1] This vital interest in the frontier West remained with him throughout his life, impelling him in *American and Americans* to validate traditional mythic conceptions of the nation's Western heritage. He writes:

> The dreams of a people either create folk literature or find their way into it; and folk literature, again, is always based on something that happened. Our most persistent folk tales—constantly retold in books, movies, and television shows—concern cowboys, gunslinging sheriffs and Indian fighters. These folk figures existed—perhaps not quite as they are recalled nor in the numbers indicated, but they did exist; and this dream also persists.[2]

While a number of critics have noted Steinbeck's focus on frontier themes, several seek to distance Steinbeck from the traditional Wild West mythology he embraces above, as well as from traditional visions of pioneers' agrarian

From *Steinbeck Quarterly* 26, nos. 3 and 4 (Summer–Fall 1993): 81–90. Copyright © 1993 by *Steinbeck Quarterly*.

and westering experiences on the frontier. In "'Directionality': The Compass in the Heart," for example, John Ditsky argues that *The Grapes of Wrath* shows "mere westering leads nowhere,"[3] and Chester E. Eisinger describes "the bankruptcy of Jefferson's ideal" in "Jeffersonian Agrarianism in *The Grapes of Wrath*" and claims that "we must seek another road to the independence and security and dignity we expect from democracy."[4] Warren French argues that *Grapes* represents "an attempt . . . to explode rather than perpetuate the myths and conventions upon which Western genre fiction [is] based."[5] And in his recent study, *John Steinbeck's Re-Vision of America*, Louis Owens holds that

> Steinbeck again and again in short story and novel held the dangers of the westering myth up to view. . . . Steinbeck saw no cornucopia of democracy in the retreating frontier, but rather a destructive and even fatal illusion barring Americans from the realization of any profound knowledge of the continent they had crossed.[6]

Though these views reflect a developing critical consensus regarding Steinbeck's vision of the frontier, Steinbeck's own words in *America and Americans*, and the words of a sympathetic farmer he presents in *Travels with Charley*, who laments, "This used to be a nation of giants. Where have they gone?"[7] haunt us and call us back to reconsider the nature of Steinbeck's deeply held vision of the frontier past.

Though French has distanced Steinbeck's work from the western genre, in fact Steinbeck's preoccupations closely parallel issues central to literary western stories and novels, particularly those that examine contemporary cultural degeneration. William Bloodworth discovers in the literary western "the sense of a vanished world in which action, gesture, and character had more significance than it does [*sic*] in the present."[8] Similarly, David Lavender, citing the works of Conrad Richter and Willa Cather, describes the frequent appearance of characters plagued by "a vitiation of energy" who experience "the universal tragedy of lost strength."[9] In "Steinbeck's 'The Leader of the People': A Crisis in Style," Philip J. West describes Steinbeck's affiliation with this tradition, reflected in his depiction of the "diminished stature of society in the Salinas Valley . . . [which] is . . . hinted at in the epic devices that outlive epic greatness."[10] In fact, not only in *The Red Pony* but throughout his career, Steinbeck frequently exhibited concern that when compared to the frontier past, contemporary American life often lacks integrity and meaning, and that contemporary Americans increasingly resemble "a national kennel of animals with no purpose and no direction."[11] In delineating these deficits in culture and character, Steinbeck consistently represents the mythic frontier past and its prototypical figures—yeomen, cowboys, scouts, frontier fighters, hunters, wagonmasters, and westering pioneers—as an ideal or standard, while at the same time portraying modern characters who are, at best, diminished descendants of these idealized frontier types.

This comparative strategy appears, for example, in Steinbeck's characterization of such diverse figures as the hapless "hunter," Hubert Van Deventer, in *The Pastures of Heaven* (1932), the inept "scout," Pimples Carson, in *The Wayward Bus* (1947), and even the effete store clerk, Ethan Allen Hawley, in *The Winter of Our Discontent* (1961), who painfully recognizes the disparity between his own experience and that of his legendary ancestor.[12] Valuing the skill, self-reliance, and forthright vision of their cultural (and at times biological) forebears yet incapable of similar achievement themselves, such characters often live destructive lives that can only be described as diminished perversions of mythic frontier life. Steinbeck's effort to illuminate modern personal and cultural degeneration through reference to frontier types is also convincingly revealed in two stories from *The Long Valley* collection, "The White Quail" and "The Chrysanthemums."

In "The White Quail," Steinbeck describes the protagonist, Mary Teller, as a diminished modern yeoman who attempts to create a perfect garden in the post-frontier West. Mary's husband, Harry, contributes to this project for a time, but ultimately recognizes its perverse nature and hunts down and kills the white quail, which, in Mary's mind, symbolizes the garden's perfection. Owens argues that "Mary's garden is an attempt to construct an unfallen Eden in a fallen world, a neurotic projection of Mary's self."[13] He concludes that the story ultimately reveals "the futility of holding to the Eden myth— even the danger of the illusion."[14] In describing Mary as yeoman and Harry as hunter, however, Steinbeck does not sharply undercut the myth of agrarianism as Owens suggests. Instead, by revealing the degenerate nature of the characters' personalities and actions, Steinbeck satirizes the narcissism and pathological self-delusion that cripple the modern American imagination and reflect the culture's degeneration.

As a frontier-based narrative, Steinbeck's story achieves much of its power through the dualistic quality of its setting and characters. Steinbeck purposely sets the story on a "frontier," or borderland possessing attributes of both a wilderness and a Crèvecoeurian "middle region" to emphasize the story's thematic connection with frontier history:

> Right at the edge of the garden, the hills started up, wild with cascara bushes and poison oak, with dry grass and live oak, very wild. If you didn't go around to the front of the house, you couldn't tell it was on the very edge of town.[15]

This setting functions as a modern suburban frontier, similar in appearance to the historical frontier, but diminished in size, a kind of mock frontier.

The setting is both like the historical frontier and unlike it at the same time, just as the characters are both types and antitypes of mythic frontier figures. In her effort to tame this frontier and transform it into a garden, Mary Teller appears to be a descendant of the homesteader, or yeoman, celebrated in the agrarian myth. Yet, in actuality, Mary is a diminished yeoman whose approach to nature inverts the yeoman's traditional approach to the land. Where the pioneer yeoman saw opportunity in the wilderness and approached it with expectancy, Mary sees danger in "the dark thickets of the hill": "'That's the enemy,' Mary said one time. 'That's the world that wants to get in, all rough and tangled and unkempt'" (pp. 26–27). Where the yeoman gained strength and virtue through contact with the soil, Mary protects herself from contact with nature by wearing a "sunbonnet" and "good sturdy gloves" (p. 25), and hires workers to carry out the actual labor.

Harry joins his wife on this suburban frontier as a diminished hunter, reminiscent of the Wild West hunter in the Leatherstocking tradition, yet curiously distinct from the type as well. Like the hunter, Harry appears near the story's end as a skilled marksman more at home in the wilderness of the hill beyond the garden than in the garden itself. But in his unconsidered acquiescence to Mary's neurotic wishes, his choice of an air gun as a weapon, and his pursuit of the harmless white quail as prey, Harry becomes a ridiculous figure, scarcely resembling the self-reliant frontier hunter whose "physical strength, adaptability to nature, resourcefulness and courage"[16] defined him as a heroic type.

As the story progresses, Steinbeck intensifies the distinction between the ideals of frontier yeoman and hunter and the modern setting and characters. Robert S. Hughes, Jr., argues that in both setting and plot, the story is "unusually static."[17] Implicit in the idea of frontier development is change and progress, but here stasis becomes the ideal: "'We won't ever change it, will we Harry?' Mary begs. 'If a bush dies, we'll put another one just like it in the same place'" (p. 24). Whereas the yeoman harvested trees to build a shelter and food crops to feed a family, Mary's "harvest" consists of the sight of birds that "come to my garden for peace and for water" (p. 27), "bowls of flowers [which] were exquisite" (p. 25), and ultimately the white quail, "an essence boiled down to utter purity" (p. 33). And whereas the yeomen faced life-threatening challenges from Indians seeking to reclaim their land, droughts, floods, and fires, Mary and Harry must defend themselves against such dubious adversaries as snails and slugs:

> Mary held the flashlight while Harry did the actual killing. . . . He knew it must be a disgusting business to her, but the light never wavered. "Brave girl," he thought. "She has a sturdiness in back of that fragile beauty." (p. 26)

Near the story's end, the diminished Tellers face a final threat to their garden world in the form of a cat pursuing the quail. James C. Work argues that the white quail is a "life force,"[18] and Owens claims that the cat represents "the real world that Mary cannot keep forever from her garden."[19] Yet the Tellers' reaction to these two animals further emphasizes the protagonists' degeneration. As "an albino. No pigment in the feathers" (p. 35), the quail is indeed rare. But like the bowls of flowers and the garden itself, the quail is valued not for its genuine affinity with nature but rather for its distinctiveness, or isolation, from the "impurity" Mary imputes to the uncontrolled natural world. Similarly, though the cat is obviously a threat to the quail, it presents no real danger to the Tellers. What is significant in this minor conflict is that the Tellers elevate it to the stature of crisis, just as the snail hunt takes on exaggerated meaning earlier. The story's final episode thus becomes a testament to the Tellers' diminishment.

Harry's decision to kill the white quail, instead of the cat, at the end of the story may be seen, as Owens suggests, as an attack in frustration against "the heart of Mary's illusory garden." But Harry is not "an exile from the unreal Eden" as Owens claims.[20] Though they are at odds in their valuation of the white quail, the Tellers are much more alike in their misplaced values than they are different. As Steinbeck depicts them, they are both degenerate types: she a modern yeoman, he a modern hunter. They are Americans whose contracted imaginative vision interprets cats, slugs, and snails as adversaries to be destroyed, and whose unproductive suburban pleasure gardens provide meaningless challenges that ironically prove insurmountable. In their effort to create a "pure" landscape to mirror Mary's obsessive preconceptions and to give them both sensate pleasure, the Tellers lose perspective and forfeit any authentic relationship with the complex reality of nature and with each other. Their world is, as Owens argues, "an emotional wasteland without any certain hope for fructification, spiritual or physical."[21] Through this satire on modern western "settlement," Steinbeck exposes the suburban frontier and its "settlers," and questions what remains in American character of the physical capability and expansive vision of the West's pioneers.

In "The Chrysanthemums," a second story in *The Long Valley* collection, Steinbeck again addresses the issue of cultural degeneration, this time in connection with the idea of westering. Work argues that "Elisa's life [on the foothill ranch] is dull, repetitive and vaguely frustrating," whereas "the itinerant tinker who pulls up to her fence one afternoon is a virile life-force who comes into her closed valley, arouses and confuses her emotions, and leaves."[22] Owens agrees with Work's assessment of Elisa's situation, claiming that "Elisa is seeking symbols of commitment in a world of physical, spiritual, and emotional isolation and sterility,"[23] a world revitalized in the story by "the fertilizing imagination of the tinker."[24] As Hughes persuasively argues, however, the tinker is a self-serving character who "lives for his own pleasure."[25] French identifies him as an "unscrupulous confidence man," and reads the story as an indictment against "the manipulation of people's dreams for selfish purposes."[26]

In contrast to the tinker's ambiguous character, Elisa can be seen as the truly vital life force in the story. Although her frustration with the limitations placed on her by her situation causes her to find the tinker's life attractive, Elisa's authentic connection to the earth validates her own life and serves as a strong contrast to the basic deception practiced by the tinker. The tinker, far from being a symbol of vitality, is rather a symbol of the degeneration of westering mythic energies, which were founded on acts of discovery and exploration. Although troubling in its apparent denigration of Elisa's situation, in actuality, the story celebrates her authentic connection to a realistic garden and reveals through the character of the tinker the absence of significant direction or purpose that debilitates modern American culture.

The story opens in late autumn, traditionally associated with the decline of the year and here symbolic of cultural decline as well.[27] In his portrayal of Elisa, Steinbeck creates an image of a person at home in nature, comfortable in a garden of her own making, and free of the neuroses that plague Mary Teller:

> Her face was eager and mature and handsome.... She brushed a cloud of hair out of her eyes with the back of her glove, and left a smudge of earth on her cheek in doing it. Behind her stood the neat white farm house with red geraniums close banked around it as high as the windows. (p. 4)

In tending her garden, Elisa has "a gift with things," Steinbeck writes, "planter's hands that knew" how to work in concert with nature's seasonal cycles (p. 5). Although critics often emphasize the sterility of Elisa's life, in fact, she operates, in contrast to both her husband and the tinker, as a vital force that maintains the yeoman's idealized connection with the land.

The tinker contrasts sharply with Elisa, functioning as a symbol of both personal and cultural degeneration. Steinbeck emphasizes the importance of this figure as a symbolic descendant of the westering pioneers by placing him at the reins of an anachronistic vehicle, "an old spring-wagon, with a round canvas top on it like the cover of a prairie schooner" (p. 7). Elisa and her husband own a roadster. The tinker enters the scene, then, as an important symbol of frontier westering that seems to emerge again on a post-frontier landscape. Yet degeneration, not vitality, distinguishes this modern westerer, who becomes an antitype of the pioneers. His condition reflects both his own degenerate moral "vision," which neither values Elisa's patient nurturing of the land and gift of chrysanthemum sprouts nor exhibits any scruples about deceptively manipulating her emotions, and the decay of a central, once-grand westering tradition. Steinbeck highlights the disjunction between the tinker and the pioneers through his description of the wagon:

> Elisa . . . watched to see the crazy, loose-jointed wagon pass by. But it didn't pass. It turned into the farm road in front of her house, crooked old wheels skirling and squeaking. . . . Words were painted on the canvas, in clumsy, crooked letters. "Pots, pans, knives, sisors, lawn mores, Fixed." Two rows of articles, and the triumphantly definitive "Fixed" below. The black paint had run down in little sharp points beneath each letter. (p. 7)

Reminiscent in shape only of the frontier settlers who pioneered the vast reaches of the continent and etched their destination and the epic stature of their adventure—"California or Bust"—on their canvases, the tinker and his rig, trade, and lack of direction all point symbolically to his degenerate state as a diminished descendant of the pioneers. In marked contrast to Elisa's vibrant flowers, the tinker's "horse and . . . donkey drooped like unwatered flowers" (p. 7), and unlike the westerers Grandfather celebrates in "The Leader of the People," the tinker has no destination, no purpose or goal in mind: "I ain't in any hurry, ma'am. I go from Seattle to San Diego and back every year. Takes all my time. About six months each way. I aim to follow nice weather'" (p. 8). Roads and the places they lead figure prominently throughout Steinbeck's fiction. By contrasting the tinker's journey with the mythic westering trek in terms of both its directionality and relative significance of purpose, Steinbeck argues that not only this representative man but much of the culture is off its "general road," its historical road of destiny (p. 8). Unlike the pioneers, whose linear movement became a metaphor for both personal and cultural progress, this modern-day westerer simply travels in circles, not building a new culture but patching up the old, broken, worn-out one symbolized in the pots and pans he repairs.

The great irony of "The Chrysanthemums" is that a woman of tremendous vitality and connection with the natural world would be attracted to the aimless life of the tinker. Some critics argue that the narrowness of Elisa's life, symbolized by the fog-shrouded farm that resembles a "closed pot" in Steinbeck's opening description (p. 1), prompts her to idealize the tinker's carefree existence. Though Elisa's life clearly is not entirely satisfying, she seems nevertheless to misapprehend the truly bankrupt nature of the tinker's life. "'That's a bright direction. There's a glowing there'" (p. 14), Elisa comments as the tinker departs, and through her gift of chrysanthemum sprouts she vicariously joins him on his circuitous route. But the trip into town undeceives her, for on the roadside she discovers her discarded chrysanthemums, symbol of her earth-based vitality, cast aside by the tinker, providing ample evidence, in Owens's words, of "the tinker's broken faith."[28]

Here Steinbeck clearly indicates that despite Elisa's dissatisfaction with human relationships in her life, her connection with the earth, a realistic yet beautiful garden, is authentic, just as her gift of chrysanthemums is authentic and vital. The life of the tinker, on the other hand, lacks physical, moral, and spiritual direction. By consciously manipulating Elisa's fascination with the pioneer spirit of freedom and adventure—in fact, by fraudulently posing as the modern embodiment of that spirit—simply to increase his trade, the tinker crushes Elisa's vital nature and destroys the momentary emotional and psychic pleasure she experiences by vicariously joining the tinker on his "adventurous" journey. Through his depiction of the tinker as a degenerate modern descendant of the westering pioneers, Steinbeck contrasts the aimlessness of modern American culture with the purpose and accomplishment of the westering heritage in American history. In his intrusion and despoilment of Elisa's imperfect but significantly productive and life-giving garden, the tinker becomes for Steinbeck a dark portrait of modern America's physical and transcendentally spiritual distance from its agrarian and westering past, a figure entirely lacking any respect for Elisa's wholesome connection with her land or a supra-material, visionary conception of personal or cultural advancement and progress.

Like *Travels with Charley*, *America and Americans*, and *The Wayward Bus*, among others, "The White Quail" and "The Chrysanthemums" reveal an important dimension of Steinbeck's fascinating, often paradoxical vision of America's frontier heritage. Whereas Ditsky, Owens, and French emphasize Steinbeck's self-distancing from traditional frontier mythology and history, here we see his appropriation of that legacy as a kind of ideal against which to measure contemporary American culture. Perhaps the greatest significance of these two stories, in addition to their thematic embrace of frontier ideals, is their date of publication; for although it may be argued that Steinbeck's celebration of the frontier past in *Travels with Charley* and *America and Americans* represents the nostalgic musings of an aging writer, these stories appeared, of course, as Steinbeck neared the pinnacle of his artistic powers in the thirties, indicating an early (and enduring) fascination with the mythic frontier West not yet fully appreciated.

Notes

1. Jackson J. Benson, *The True Adventures of John Steinbeck, Writer* (New York: Viking Press, 1984), 138, 134.

2. John Steinbeck, *America and Americans* (New York: Viking Press, 1966), 33–34.

3. John Ditsky, "'Directionality': The Compass in the Heart," *The Westering Experience in American Literature, Bicentennial Essays* (Bellingham, Washington: Bureau for Faculty Research, Western Washington University, 1977), 219.

4. Chester E. Eisinger, "Jeffersonian Agrarianism in *The Grapes of Wrath*," *A Casebook on "The Grapes of Wrath,"* ed. Agnes McNeill Donohue (New York: Thomas Y. Crowell, 1968), 150.

5. Warren French, "Another Look at *The Grapes of Wrath*," *A Companion to "The Grapes of Wrath,"* ed. Warren French (Clifton, New Jersey: Augustus M. Kelley Publishers, 1972), 222.

6. Louis Owens, *John Steinbeck's Re-Vision of America* (Athens: University of Georgia Press, 1985), 4.

7. John Steinbeck, *Travels with Charley in Search of America* (New York: Bantam Doubleday Dell, 1963), 168.

8. William Bloodworth, "Literary Extensions of the Formula Western," *Western American Literature* 14 (Winter 1980), 295.

9. David Lavender, "The Petrified West and the Writer," *American Scholar* 37 (Spring 1968), 301–302.

10. Philip J. West, "Steinbeck's 'The Leader of the People': A Crisis in Style," *Western American Literature* 5 (Summer 1970), 140.

11. Steinbeck, *America and Americans*, 139.

12. John Steinbeck, *The Pastures of Heaven* (New York: Viking Press, 1932); *The Wayward Bus* (New York: Viking Press, 1947); *The Winter of Our Discontent* (New York: Viking Press, 1961).

13. Owens, *Re-Vision*, 113.

14. *Ibid.*, 114–115.

15. John Steinbeck, "The White Quail," in *The Long Valley* (1938) (New York: Viking Penguin, 1986), 21. Subsequent citations refer to this edition.

16. Delbert E. Wylder, "The Western Novel as Literature of the Last Frontier," *The Frontier Experience and the American Dream*, eds. David Mogen *et al.* (College Station, Texas: Texas A&M University Press, 1989), 121.

17. Robert S. Hughes, Jr., *Beyond the Red Pony: A Reader's Companion to Steinbeck's Complete Short Stories* (Metuchen, New Jersey: Scarecrow Press, 1987), 63.

18. James C. Work, "Coordinate Forces in 'The Leader of the People,'" *Western American Literature* 16 (Winter 1982), 280.

19. Owens, *Re-Vision*, 114.

20. *Ibid.*, 116.

21. *Ibid.*

22. Work, "Coordinate Forces," 280.

23. Owens, *Re-Vision*, 112.

24. *Ibid.*, 109.

25. Hughes, *Companion*, 61.

26. Warren French, *John Steinbeck* (New York: Twayne Publishers, 1961), 83.

27. John Steinbeck, "The Chrysanthemums," in *The Long Valley* (1938), (New York: Viking Penguin, 1986), 3. Subsequent citations refer to this edition.

28. Owens, *Re-Vision*, 112.

JOHN DITSKY

"Your Own Mind Coming Out in the Garden": Steinbeck's Elusive Woman

During the period in which John Steinbeck wrote the three Depression novels that are the special focus of this Third International Steinbeck Congress, he also published one other notable volume of fiction: the memorable assemblage of short stories collectively entitled *The Long Valley*.[1] Few readers or critics of Steinbeck would argue with the claim that these four volumes represent Steinbeck at his best. But as Robert S. Hughes, Jr., noted in his paper for the Tenth Salinas Steinbeck Festival in August 1989,[2] there are very different orientations in Steinbeck's short fiction as opposed to his novels, with the differences being bridged perhaps only in the hybrid work *The Pastures of Heaven*. Moreover, little of *The Long Valley* has anything to do with the struggles of the American worker, the preoccupation of the novels that are our subject.

Tetsumaro Hayashi, our director, originally suggested a paper on Steinbeck criticism as it is today and as it will be in the future. But I feel I exhausted my powers as sage and guru when I did much the same sort of thing in 1988 at the Ninth Salinas Steinbeck Festival. And the future of Steinbeck criticism is rapidly passing into younger hands that have no need of my powers of prophecy. I would therefore like to speak about parts of *The Long Valley* in a way that expands upon the observations I made in Salinas in 1988, and also springs from some of what I had to say in the same city a year later. In

From *John Steinbeck: The Years of Greatness, 1936–1939*, edited by Tetsumaro Hayashi, pp. 3–19, 165–67. Copyright © 1993 by the University of Alabama Press.

75

so doing, I would like to try to pin down some of the characteristic means by which Steinbeck, as though he were a writer of detective fiction, made a life-long quest of understanding that elusive thing called Woman—and perhaps, like most of us, failed.

The most prominent of Steinbeck's feminist critics is certainly Mimi Reisel Gladstein, who has written with conviction about Steinbeck's "indestructible" females, as well as about the apparent "misogyny" *The Wayward Bus* evidences.[3] More recently, she has also written about the curious anomaly by which Steinbeck, who knew so many remarkable women in his life, fails to recreate them in his own fiction.[4] Gladstein fairly admits that the autonomy of the artist includes the right to do precisely that if he chooses, but she just as rightly raises the issue of the peculiarity of the situation. The Depression novels clearly prove that Steinbeck's depiction of events on the picket lines and at the hiring tables does not reflect the "actual" presence of charismatic women at those scenes in the "real" 1930s. With the classic exception of the "indestructible" Ma Joad, the women in *In Dubious Battle*, *Of Mice and Men*, and *The Grapes of Wrath* are apt to be either sad or silly—or both. But in *The Long Valley*, as Susan Shillinglaw has recently been proving, women—or the Woman—come into their own, albeit a bit at a time.[5] That this quest for the nature of Woman occupied Steinbeck for a lifetime is a subject beyond the scope of this chapter. That certain key stories in *The Long Valley* speak to the issue is what I intend to address.

In the three labor novels being discussed during this congress, the world of action is the world of men, with the women surrendering their relative passivity only in the third volume of the trilogy, if we can call it that, *The Grapes of Wrath*. There, it is true, Ma's assumption of the "male" function of action does come to represent the potential for revolutionary change in the human family, but its highest and most notorious achievement is the closing tableau, in which revolutionary action can also be said to be passion of a sort. Indeed, what Rose of Sharon participates in is a curious kind of act of love that has reminded some readers, myself included, of the results of another Passion, the biblical one, in its culmination in a version of the Pietà.[6] Woman here has not yet succeeded in moving out of her mythical and archetypal role; rather, she has simply stretched it a bit.

Hughes pointed out in Salinas that while the novels focus on society, the short stories deal with individual psychology. It is in the short stories, then, that we might expect to see women portrayed as individuals, whether or not they are confined there to doing the womanly appropriate things. In a recent issue of the *Steinbeck Quarterly*, I discuss one of the stories from *The Long Valley*, "The Murder," in which Woman is truly presented as the unfathomable Other, with her nearly species difference conveyed by Jelka's being a member of the Slavic race.[7] I also suggest that there is ambiguity in "The Murder" over whether Jim Moore's point of view, in its failure to understand womankind, is not also characteristic of Steinbeck himself. It may be significant that the last two stories in *The Long Valley* before the *Red Pony* pieces deal in a way with womankind: "The Murder," with its aforementioned ambiguities; and "St. Katy the Virgin," which I am not for a moment going to risk considering as a commentary on the female sex—though I did wake up in the middle of the night recently with the troubling question of whether St. Katy, that nasty little porker, might at least subconsciously have served as the model for Cathy Ames.

I

I am not about to deal with those stories in which Steinbeck may be throwing up his hands at the impossibility of understanding women, any more than I wish to deal with the symbolic implications of the collection's title, which just may allude to the existence of a patient, everlasting, and naturally female *place* where Man—male horse, male rider—thinks he is free to act. I want to deal with those three of the first four stories in the collection that attempt to answer the question "What is Woman?": "The Chrysanthemums," "The White Quail," and "The Snake." These stories have been extensively analyzed before, and I do not expect to be able to do much that is truly novel with them here, but perhaps I will be able to glean something from them that can take our thinking in a new direction.

Many of us have written about "The Chrysanthemums," surely the most often anthologized of Steinbeck's pieces, but few of us have wholly agreed. Like the other stories under consideration today, its ambiguities are centered in the mystery of Woman herself, but unlike the others, it pretends to a sympathy the others do not possess. Interestingly, however, what might strike a male reader as Steinbeck's most "feminist" piece of fiction does not seem to evoke the same response among women. In a recent class of mine, the women were deeply divided over the issue of whether Elisa Allen is a sympathetic figure or not. It would seem that more than half a century after the writing of "The Chrysanthemums," women are impatient with a character who appears to be unable or unwilling to do anything about her own perceived state of entrapment.

But Elisa's entrapment is deeply rooted in character, and her psychology is complicated by the fact that she both dresses and addresses her work in her garden in a mannish fashion. Furthermore, in her encounter with the tinker, it is the freedom of his man's life on the road that appeals to her as much as, if not more than, his maleness. I have written recently about the theatricality of this story,[8] and I would extend my remarks now by observing that Elisa is manipulated by the tinker into playing the female role, finding him some

work to do and thus catering to his maleness, before he will complete the pretended transaction by accepting her unwanted flowers—which he, of course,
abandons heartlessly. It is on the strength of this bit of dramatic self-delusion
that Elisa indulges in her narcissistic cleansing, admiring, and adorning of
her body. Her bewildered husband, Henry, noting the results, inadvertently
but accurately describes them as "a kind of play." But he also describes what
he sees as "strong," a curious term to use to describe a woman in the full flush
of womanhood—that is, a woman fully possessed of stereotypical womanli-
ness. Elisa is enough of a person by this time—a woman with a man's sense
of freedom—that she can even consider going with Henry to the fights, and
one can only guess what rewards poor Henry might have reaped later had
she indeed gone. But only moments after the not-unexpected finding of the
discarded chrysanthemums along the road, Elisa subsides into a state of "crying weakly—like an old woman." It is a tribute to the perceptiveness of Steinbeck's presentation of the equivocal nature of human sexuality to note that
after half a century or more, we have not by any means run out of things to
say about this little story.

But no single Steinbeck story is able to express the ambiguities of the
writer's attitudes towards Woman. Her mysteriousness would remain largely
unfathomable to him until, perhaps, quite late in his career. To enlarge upon
a point made earlier, we remember that Steinbeck's greatest novel ends with
an awestruck visit to a shrine to femaleness, and that the book's last word is
"mysteriously," referring to Rose of Sharon's smile.[9] The mystery of femaleness presented in "The Chrysanthemums" is approached from another angle
in "The White Quail." Again, the female character is so preoccupied with her
long-planned garden that she chooses her husband on the basis of whether
or not the garden will "like" him (*TLV* [*The Long Valley*], p. 28). When her
choice lights on Harry Teller, her beauty makes him "hungry," but access to
her "untouchable" nature depends on his compliant acceptance of the importance of her garden to her, for he recognizes—in the line which is the title of
this paper—that the garden is the expression of her psychology (p. 29). But
her mind, when it comes "out in the garden," is a curious one indeed, for she
talks about the garden "almost as though she were talking about herself," and
yet when she refers to a particular fuchsia tree—part of the garden that is
herself—she calls it "he" (p. 31). This "he" is meant to protect the garden from
intrusion from the wild world without; "pretty" Mary is not bothered by the
process of destroying "slugs and snails" for her garden's sake, and she is willing to poison an intruding cat to preserve what is meant to be a bird sanctu-
ary (pp. 31–32). Harry wonders what is going on inside her "cool, collected
mind," but Mary indicates that she may not be what he thinks he sees; indeed,
when she looks indoors from outside one evening, she finds herself "seeing"

herself through the window, and she admires what she sees—and also the ability to appreciate her doubleness (pp. 33–34). But she cannot reveal herself to Harry on this score, for that would ruin things; her mind is as spoilable as her garden.

The secret garden of Mary's mind is thus preserved from infiltration in the same way she withholds her body from Harry when he cannot understand her attempts to prettify his man's world of business ethics. Later, when Harry has the temerity to crave an Irish terrier puppy, Mary's "curse of imagination" causes her to become feverish with a psychosomatic headache. One notes here, and with interest, the connecting of the power to imagine with the sexuality of the female, even to the extent of punishment by denial of sex—not to mention the proverbial headache that accompanies the denial, if not as part of the same incident then at least as part of the same page of narrative (*TLV*, p. 36).

One dusk, which Mary considers her "really-garden-time," a "little white hen quail" appears in her garden, and Mary immediately concludes—rather remarkably—that the quail is "like the essence of me, an essence boiled down to utter purity" (*TLV*, p. 38). The quail brings Mary memories of a ritual three "ecstasies," a sequence of moments in which her imagination stood poised on the threshold of experiences new to her: candy she mustn't taste, praise for her patience "like a gentian," and news of her father's death (p. 39). Mary's inhumanly protracted "purity," embodied in the quail, is next seen as threatened by a cat, and Harry's refusal to use poison against "animals in my garden" brings on predictable results: the headache, the locked bedroom door. Harry promises to shoot the cat with his air rifle to scare it off and thus protect what Mary calls "the secret me that no one can ever get at" (p. 41). Instead, he kills the quail, of course, though he tells himself he just wanted to scare it away, and he buries it outside the garden. Interestingly, the story switches focus at its ending to Harry; having killed his wife's "secret me," he blames himself and bemoans his loneliness.

Mary Teller can be called a pathological, grown child or what you will, but the salient fact of her story's narration is that it changes sides. At its ending, the male figure accepts his fate: he will never get inside his wife's mind and soul, and the story has already suggested that his access to her body may be at an end. The otherness of Woman has been confirmed again, as mystified men are left outside the garden with the unruly elements of existence: cats, dogs, horses, and tinker's dams. The balance of empathy seems to have shifted: the last words of "The Chrysanthemums" are "old woman," but those of "The White Quail" are a man's wailed "I'm so lonely!" (*TLV*, p. 42). The stories tally, however, in terms of the presentation of Woman as mysteriously possessed of the ability to order the garden of herself through the powers of the imagination. In the process, we have also moved closer to the narrative form of the parable.

Parabolic form is approached even more closely in "The Snake," the third of the stories on Woman under consideration. In it, the mystery of Woman is heightened by the fact that Steinbeck makes use of (but alters) an incident that took place in Ed Rickett's lab to present supposedly objective observations in a supposedly objective milieu. The woman in this story has no name, however; she is neither Allen nor Teller. She is a case history: something that happened. She enters a scientist's domain with a special request—to purchase a snake and watch it feed. We learn nothing about her but her gender. But in the process, she becomes a species watching another species—Woman watching reptile—and thereby she also becomes an intermediate subject for observation: she becomes Woman being watched by Man watching a reptile consume a rat. Man, the reader presumably included, is thus tempted to stand back and annotate the proceedings. In effect, she offers herself, albeit unintentionally, as datum.

Putting things another way, this is the third in a sequence of fictional relationships between men and women. Like Mary Teller's husband, Dr. Phillips recognizes through his experience with his woman visitor that he is lonely—"alone," as the story puts it. The same recognition would come to Doc in *Sweet Thursday*, but before what most readers take to be a sentimentalized, hence improbable, mating ritual. In the two laboratory stories, however, the objective scientist is made to discover his aloneness through contact with the other "species," Woman. Dr. Phillips is introduced as being methodical in his life and work, which are inseparable as routines from one another. He will stroke a cat moments before coolly putting it to death to become a science exhibit. The woman, when she arrives, is not interested in his preparation of slides; indeed, her presence causes him to abort a preparation sequence. The dispassionate technician is moved by the sight of the woman to want to "shock" her and reach her; in fact, the operative word is "arouse" (*TLV*, p. 77). Her apparent passivity is the motivation—something he thinks must signal a low metabolic rate, "almost as low as a frog's." As the story progresses, the woman's black, seemingly unfocused eyes seem to become "dusty," the word used to describe Jelka's in "The Murder" (pp. 77–78, 86).

Many have noted the empathy between woman and snake, something Steinbeck heightens for artistic purposes, partially by having Dr. Phillips be alone with the woman. No other male observers are present, which apparently was also the case in the real-life basis for the story; thus the woman's imitation of the snake's movements—which Steinbeck avoids having to make truly bizarre by having Phillips turn away while the snake devours the rat— takes on a semblance of the grotesque that it might not otherwise possess for anyone who has bottle-fed an infant and observed his or her own imitative response. Phillips had expected empathy for the rat, not the snake, but the woman has surprised him, and he feels almost a moral revulsion for what he has allowed to occur, for he objects to making sport of "natural processes." The killing of the snake is to the scientist "the most beautiful thing in the world," "the most terrible thing in the world" (*TLV*, p. 83). This is that "burning bright" force of life and death in the universe which Man may worship and measure; Woman simply embodies it naturally—as the Other.

It should be remembered that the woman specifically requests a *male* snake as her surrogate, a snake that, when it is about to devour its prey, almost seems to "kiss" the rat's body (*TLV*, pp. 78–79, 84). In "The Murder," communication between the genders is achieved in a way—through violence—but the three stories under discussion are united by sexual ambivalence, and repressed sexuality expresses itself through the male, the animal, and even the aggressor. As a scientist, Phillips is capable of criticizing this anecdote as literature, like Ethan Allen Hawley's self-conscious posturings as Jesus and Judas. But all he has read about what he calls "psychological sex symbols" does not help him understand the mystery of Woman. Clearly, this man who intended to shock and arouse has himself been sexually troubled—attracted and repulsed—by his visitor, whom he vows to leave to her practices "alone," but for whom he then searches the streets of his town for "months" afterward, never again encountering her (p. 86). "The Snake" is thus what the movies used to call a "different kind of love story."

It is notable that Steinbeck wrote these stories while he was married to his first wife, Carol, surely a remarkable woman even in a life rife with remarkable women. But my purposes are not those of biographical speculation. I am interested in the way in which, as these stories appear in *The Long Valley* one after another, the stage slowly turns 180 degrees until Man, not Woman, is downstage, and the audience has to look a distance upstage to see Woman through his eyes. In such extended works as *The Grapes of Wrath* and *The Wayward Bus* Steinbeck shows the spheres of activity of men and women as separate worlds with separate rituals, practices, and arcana. Yet Steinbeck, as I noted in my paper for the Tenth Salinas Steinbeck Festival in 1989,[10] regularly referred to his work in the writing of *Grapes* as "she" or "her." This is usage common to men who, like Juan Chicoy in *Bus*, work on the engines of automobiles and buses. But Steinbeck's text is as lubriciously female as any that might titillate and tantalize such a critic as the late Roland Barthes.[11] As I have also noted before, Steinbeck's muse was clearly a woman. Hence his artistry is a love affair of sorts, and if we wish to find the embodiment of the remarkable (if Other) Woman he knew in "real life," it is in his art that we must seek it, or her.

II

In *The Pastures of Heaven*, Steinbeck described an Edenic landscape that inspired the men who set eyes upon it with the vain ambition to impose their wills upon it. That this landscape is described in feminine terms is as evident there as it is in *The Long Valley*. The stories we have been looking at, with their two gardens and a snake, suggest that the locus of the discovery of the knowledge of good and evil is a feminized Edenic landscape, and that within that landscape men struggle to understand their destinies—destinies altered by the appearance of Woman in their midst. To strain the analogy just a bit more, it could be argued that moral struggle in Steinbeck's fiction is in a very real sense an Adamic attempt to tame—or *name*, and thus subdue—Woman, or womanly ambiguity. A recent student of mine has shown quite forcefully, for instance, that in that very moral and final Steinbeck novel *The Winter of Our Discontent*, Ethan Allen Hawley is saved by discovering, in his daughter, Ellen, the synthesis of the values represented by wife Mary and seductress Margie Young-Hunt.[12] In *East of Eden*, the moral quandary of Cathy Ames is "solved" by Abra, in an extension of the same sort of thinking. But this is to go even beyond the identification of Woman with setting, or even with plot. It is to argue the oneness of Woman and Steinbeck's art itself.

Within that oneness, however, exists a duality that may at first escape the reader's attention. In whatever manner these stories show Woman as Other, the fact that men do not understand them whether or not they seek to is not enough of a commonality to generalize further. The conventionalized lives of Elisa Allen and Mary Teller are in differing degrees the products of their own doing, expressed, as with the very different woman in "The Snake," as gender confusion. The latter woman expresses that confusion, however, not merely by means of emulation of the *male* but by imitation of the *animal* as well. It could be argued that many of Steinbeck's males are so domesticated that in a time more oriented toward strictly gender-determined role-playing, they—not the women—stood a great risk of being accused of being the repositories of normalcy, the ones someone like Huck Finn might have feared would "sivilize" him. I realize that I am putting a cosmetic face on a process of taming that others would prefer to blame on the women, but it is often the women in Steinbeck who *dare*, even when they fail to conquer when they stoop. They dare by straining against the traces they find themselves in, or, to put it biblically, they kick against the pricks—or their husbands. Some of them delve into animality to reach for a new stage of evolution. Consider Jelka from "The Murder"; include her and her husband's descriptions of her in animal terms, for example, and you just might have to accommodate a woman whose intentions of getting her husband's attentions on her own terms could reach the extreme of bringing about the slaying of her cousin. Jelka's accommodation with her husband can be put on a level with that of "Jerry and the Dog" in Albee's *Zoo Story*, but it is also a leap beyond the norm of behavior that shocks and staggers us—like the ending of *The Grapes of Wrath* or *Burning Bright*.

In this sense, many of Steinbeck's women can be seen, if not as extraordinary individuals in the career sense, at least as what the jargon of another field of study might term "facilitators"—those who make it possible for others, especially men, to advance to new levels of comprehension, or community. When the men are reduced to drawing lines in the dirt, the women are seizing jackhammers—and baring their breasts to strangers. Two of my former students, Judy Wedeles and Beth Everest, have pointed to the surprising centrality of women in *East of Eden*, including—seemingly irrelevantly—by flying in the air.[13] The willingness to be gravid, but not bound by gravity, seems another and perhaps fairer way of characterizing Steinbeck's women. To put things another way, though these women often do not play by the rules, they manage to achieve *autonomy*. They do so without bothering to consult with the men, and, of course, that leaves the men mystified and uncertain. It is in this sense that I suggest that Steinbeck's approach to his art resembles the way he presents his women. They are the art *and* the women, up to God-knows-what in the powder room; they are Delphic and arcane and beyond control. They are autonomous and will likely change on a man at any moment. They are, in effect, *process*.

Men's work and women's work are often kept separate in Steinbeck, most notably in *The Wayward Bus*. I am not suggesting the contrary, but something closer to the notion that "man's work" *is* Woman. "She" is unpredictable and apt to follow her own lead no matter what plans the man has made for her. He may sharpen his pencils of a morning and write his intentions in a journal to his editor, but that does not predict that his work will obey his wishes; rather, he will obey *it*. In a letter to Dennis Murphy edited and introduced by Robert DeMott, Steinbeck wrote that "your only weapon is your work."[14] But he also advised Murphy to keep his work "pure and innocent and fierce." That is an interesting sequence of adjectives, and one that might seem to make no sense in the normal scheme of things. To some married men, however, including Steinbeck, they might very well seem to be the description of a wife.

In his introduction to the Murphy letter DeMott notes that Steinbeck described his "words" as his "children," and surely this notion is also worth pursuing critically. Certainly, the Murphy letter does end by describing "creativeness" as "precious stuff" of which the world has very little. But if, without stretching things too far, I can use this almost Whitmanesque terminology to refer to the finished books as the author's seed, I can just as well refer to the creative act itself in sexual terms. The work is to be "pure and innocent and fierce," but the work is also one's "only weapon." Steinbeck was involved in his never-to-be-finished Arthurian project when he wrote to Murphy, and indeed, there is a palpable tone of knightly questing about the letter. I don't doubt, therefore, that when Steinbeck speaks of a "weapon" he is subconsciously thinking of a sword, and when and if he does, he is also introducing more sexual ambivalence into his imagination of a "female" body of writing. The results of this ambivalence are the same as they are in the short stories, for when the writer has performed well, Steinbeck tells Murphy, it is because he has been able to preserve his "holy loneliness." So the holiness of the love object transfers to the creator, but in the process he becomes isolated and aware of his incompleteness.

Interestingly, Ernest Hemingway was at work on what eventually was published as *The Garden of Eden* while Steinbeck was working on the Arthurian project and writing the letter to Murphy. That novel about sexual ambivalence may remind us of the Eden story in Genesis, where the acquisition of the knowledge of good and evil is customarily associated with the realization of sexual identity, after which the Garden is closed off to the honeymoon couple and guarded by an angel with a fiery sword. East of Eden, however, the human race goes on, and considerably more creatively. I spoke above of the husband-wife analogy between the writer as Steinbeck sees "him" and "his" work. Certainly Steinbeck was recovering from contentious marriages to two exceptional women when he wrote those lines, and it is not surprising that he would naturally think of a creative relationship as an adversarial one.

To Steinbeck, apparently, the art of fiction was tantamount to a domestic argument. Somewhere along the line, the work was sure to develop a mind of its, or her, own, an appendage not at all in the cards in the beginning. Sooner or later it would want to "have its own head," something not unlike having its mind "coming out in the garden." The writer's capitulation to the autonomy of his own works is hardly unique, but his candor about the process may nearly be. In his tentative dedication of *East of Eden* to Pat Covici, Steinbeck refers to the period during which a writer is with his book as a time when they are "friends or bitter enemies but very close as only love and fighting can accomplish."[15] Early in the *Eden* journal, he developed the gender aspect of this notion at length:

> I do indeed seem to feel creative juices rushing toward an outlet as semen gathers from the four quarters of a man and fights its way into the vesicle. I hope something beautiful and true comes out—but this I know (and the likeness to coition still holds). . . . It seems to me that different organisms must have their separate ways of symbolizing, with sound or gesture, the creative joy—the

flowering.... The joy thing in me has two outlets: one a fine charge of love toward the incredibly desirable body and sweetness of woman, and second—mostly both—the paper and pencil or pen.[16]

Moments later, his "mind blasted ... with an idea so comely, like a girl, so very sweet and dear that I will put her aside for the book. Oh! she is lovely, this idea."[17] As said above, this way of relating to one's creative work is not unique to Steinbeck, though possibly the intensity described may be; indeed, the word "comely" here may remind us of the ardor expressed in the Song of Solomon, in which case it is only mildly farfetched to say that for Steinbeck, the work *is* the Rose of Sharon.

Putting himself down on the left-hand pages of the *Eden* journal, Steinbeck then went on to set down on the right-hand sheets Woman, his work. The day's work done, the journal closed, the two lay together in the dark. My quest for Steinbeck's elusive Woman has not been meant to seem a glib response to Gladstein's salient questioning about the absence of remarkable women in Steinbeck's work. Rather, it suggests one means of answering her concerns by noting one way in which his work mirrors the life he lived, for if the twinned creative outlets for Steinbeck's "juices" were Woman and work, then ultimately Steinbeck's elusive and remarkable Woman is the work herself.

Notes

1. John Steinbeck, *The Long Valley* (New York: Viking Press, 1938). Hereinafter identified as *TLV*.

2. Robert S. Hughes, Jr., "A Form Most Congenial to His Talents: Steinbeck, the Short Story, and The Pastures of Heaven," in press, *San Jose Studies*.

3. See Mimi Reisel Gladstein, *The Indestructible Woman in Faulkner, Hemingway, and Steinbeck* (Ann Arbor, Mich.: UMI Research Press, 1986), and Bobbi Gonzales and Mimi Reisel Gladstein, "*The Wayward Bus:* Steinbeck's Misogynistic Manifesto," in *Rediscovering Steinbeck: Revisionist Views of His Art, Politics and Intellect*, ed. Cliff Lewis and Carroll Britch (Lewiston, N.Y.: Edward Mellen Press, 1989), pp. 157–73.

4. Mimi Reisel Gladstein, "Women in the Migrant Labor Movement," in press, *San Jose Studies* (1989 San Jose *The Grapes of Wrath* Conference paper).

5. Susan Shillinglaw, "'The Chrysanthemums': Steinbeck's Pygmalion," in *Steinbeck's Short Stories in "The Long Valley": Essays in Criticism*, ed. Tetsumaro Hayashi. Steinbeck Monograph Series, no. 15 (Muncie, Ind.: Steinbeck Research Institute, Ball State University, 1991), pp. 1–9.

6. See my "The Ending of *The Grapes of Wrath:* A Further Commentary," *Agora* 2 (Fall 1973): 41–50, reprinted in my *Critical Essays on Steinbeck's "The Grapes of Wrath"* (Boston: G. K. Hall & Co., 1989), pp. 116–24.

7. See my "Steinbeck's 'Slav Girl' and the Role of the Narrator in 'The Murder,'" *Steinbeck Quarterly* 22 (Summer–Fall 1989): 68–76.

8. See my "'A Kind of Play': Dramatic Elements in John Steinbeck's 'The Chrysanthemums,'" *Wascana Review* 21 (Spring 1986): 62–72.

9. I take my cue from Leslie Fiedler, "Looking Back After 50 Years," *San Jose Studies* 16 (Winter 1990): 54–64.

10. See my "The Late John Steinbeck: Dissonance in the Post-*Grapes* Era," *San Jose Studies* 18 (Winter 1992): 20–32.

11. In this connection, an anecdote from recent experience seems appropriate. In October 1989 in Moscow, when Robert DeMott addressed the Moscow Writers' Union, he tried to save some time by handing a passage from *Working Days* over to our toothsome translator for direct translation into Russian. The passage had to do with the difficulty of coming to an end of the creative process. Unfortunately, due to unknown differences between Russian and English idioms, the translation began to seem to allude to other sorts of coming not unknown in English as well. In short, the audience was soon guffawing and tittering over what seemed to be Steinbeck's inability to achieve sexual satisfaction, when, in fact, simply finishing *The Grapes of Wrath* was all that was on his mind. Or was it? If the manuscript of *The Grapes of Wrath* were to have appeared to its progenitor veiled in nothing more substantial than a Freudian slip, should we be surprised?

12. Jocelyn Roberts in an unpublished paper on *The Winter of Our Discontent*.

13. Beth Everest and Judy Wedeles, "The Neglected Rib: Women in *East of Eden*," *Steinbeck Quarterly* 21 (Winter–Spring 1988): 13–23.

14. John Steinbeck, *Your Only Weapon Is Your Work*, ed. Robert DeMott (San Jose, Calif.: Steinbeck Research Center, 1985), p. 4.

15. John Steinbeck, *Journal of a Novel: The "East of Eden" Letters* (New York: Viking Press, 1969), p. 179.

16. Ibid., p. 10.

17. Ibid., p. 11.

MIMI REISEL GLADSTEIN

Faulkner and Steinbeck:
Thematic and Stylistic Resonance in the Early Stories

John Steinbeck and William Faulkner did not get off to a good start when they finally met in early 1955. Jackson Benson describes that first meeting as "disastrous," Faulkner having imbibed considerably before arriving and then sitting off by himself, not saying a word, grunting in response to questions (770). By that time Faulkner and Steinbeck were both world-famous authors, renowned novelists. The Nobel Prize had already acknowledged Faulkner's place in world literature. Steinbeck was soon to be similarly recognized. On the surface, their novelistic masterpieces could not have been more different in style, tone, characterizations, and themes. Still, a closer observation reveals both men as experimenters. Faulkner's Nobel presentation cites him as "the great experimentalist among twentieth century novelists" (5). Steinbeck was also always testing out new forms: the play-novelette, the screenplay, the travel journal. Both men were known for their sometimes-grim humor. Both were labeled early as "determinists," but the label did not stick. Seeing the similarities at the end of their careers, it is instructive to investigate some salient parallels in their early work. A generation before they first met both had published short stories that resound in resemblances.

In the early 1930s neither writer had developed enough of a reader-ship to earn a sufficient living from their writing. Faulkner, in particular, did not find short story writing especially gratifying, "his private remarks about

From *John Steinbeck and His Contemporaries*, edited by Stephen K. George and Barbara A. Heavilin, pp. 85–93. Copyright © 2007 by Stephen K. George and Barbara A. Heavilin.

87

writing short fiction for mass market magazines never stray far from two themes: scorn for the commercialism of the popular medium and cold-blooded calculation about how to take advantage of it" (Matthews 3). In 1931 *These 13*, a short story anthology that contained both "A Rose for Emily" and "Dry September" was published and sold well enough to go through a number of printings. The 1930s was also a prolific period for John Steinbeck's short story production. In 1938 *The Long Valley*, a short story anthology that included "Johnny Bear" and "The Vigilante" was published, although the two stories that are the objects of today's explication were composed as early as 1934.[1] A preliminary exploration reveals unexpected resonances between Steinbeck's "Johnny Bear" and Faulkner's "A Rose for Emily" on the one hand and Steinbeck's "The Vigilante" and Faulkner's "Dry September" on the other.

Faulkner's "A Rose for Emily" is one of the most widely anthologized and explicated of his stories.[2] From M. Thomas Inge's assessment that it is "technically distinguished" (1) to Hyatt Waggoner positioning of it as "one of the greatest written in our time" (194), there is an overwhelming consensus to its genius. Steinbeck's "Johnny Bear" does not share so illustrious a critical history. It is rarely anthologized and has been the subject of minimal critical attention. Those writers who have commented on it are often in sharp disagreement as to its quality. Although R. S. "Chip" Hughes concludes that its unsavory attitudes to do not "reflect well on its author" (85), John Timmerman finds it "one of the richest, most complex, and most powerful stories that Steinbeck wrote" (234). As part of *The Long Valley* short story anthology, it contributed to the whole, a text that drew a good deal of critical accolades, although it was seldom picked out by reviewers for special notice. The bulk of critical kudos were most often reserved for the first story "The Chrysanthemums," and the last grouping that was eventually published as *The Red Pony*.

The settings for "A Rose for Emily" and "Johnny Bear" are comparable. Each writer locates his story in the small town and rural area most closely associated with his major works. Miss Emily Grierson lives in Jefferson, a.k.a. Oxford, the county seat of Faulkner's Yoknapatawpha kingdom. The Hawkins sisters, Amy and Emalin (a name surprisingly similar to Emily) live in Loma, a small town located at the mouth of the Salinas Valley, the area now known as Steinbeck country. The fact that both stories are set in small towns is significant as both Faulkner and Steinbeck wrote often about the stultifying effects of the small town on creative or unconventional individuals. In this they may have been inspired by both their similar experiences as they battled rejection by their own communities. Faulkner early in his career was being dubbed Count No Count in Oxford and Steinbeck was considered persona non grata in both Salinas and Monterey. In addition, their anti-nostalgic recreation of small town life follows the path set by Sherwood Anderson's *Winesburg, Ohio*.

Anderson had played a key role in Faulkner's early career and *Winesburg, Ohio* was one of Steinbeck's favorite books. Jay Parini observes that Steinbeck's *The Pasture of Heaven* "has much in common" with Anderson's book (161).

Another similarity is in the choice of narrative stance. In both stories, each of these women, who is the object of her community's veneration, is not presented directly to the reader, either in the first person or by an omniscient narrator. Instead, they are presented at a distance, obliquely, as objects of spec-ulation, rarely seen. Both Faulkner and Steinbeck utilize narrators of lim-ited knowledge who present the women as viewed from afar, secreted behind closed doors, or seen through windows. This removed perspective is rein-forced by the similar choice each author makes for role of narrator. Though both narrations are first person perspectives, neither narrator is a friend or relative of the women in question. The narrators have probably not even met the subjects of their speculation. Faulkner employs an unidentified townsper-son, mostly repeating town gossip or public knowledge. He reports that Miss Emily literally closed her doors to the community and no one enters her house but her manservant, Tobe. To emphasize the distance between Miss Emily and the community, he recounts: "Now and then we would see her at a window for a moment" (127). Curiosity about Miss Emily is rampant, but the town is not even aware when she is in her final hours as they "had long since given up trying to get any information from the Negro" (128). Her lack of interaction with her peers is reinforced as the narrator explains that the women in the community came to her funeral "mostly out of curiosity to see the inside of her house" (119).

In both stories, there are no women friends for Miss Emily or the Hawkins sisters. However, there are men who are allowed into the inner sanctum of the houses that are closed to the rest of the community. Tobe, the manservant in "A Rose for Emily," seemingly supplies all of Miss Emily's needs; he is cook, gardener, butler, and housekeeper. But, the text also suggests that he is little more than a human machine. Evidence of the lack of commu-nication between him and his mistress is that, when he lets the townspeople in, after she dies, his voice "had grown harsh and rusty, as if from disuse" (129). Nor is Tobe a source of any information for the curious townspeople. After Emily's death, he lets the townspeople in and then "walked right through the house and out the back and was not seen again" (129).

In Steinbeck's story there is also one man who has access to the inner sanctum of the Hawkins' home. Steinbeck's narrative includes a doctor who is called to the Hawkins sisters' home from time to time. Though more part of the Loma community than Tobe is of Jefferson's, Doctor Holmes is bound by patient/doctor privilege and he does not provide any information. When Emalin asks if he will tell what he has seen in the house, he responds: "I'm

your doctor. . . . Of course I won't tell" (114). The Loma community's knowledge of what happens in the Hawkins place is a result of Johnny Bear's spying.

Steinbeck also makes use of an actual and symbolic divider between the
sisters and the community. A tall hedge surrounds the Hawkins' home. "Only
the roof and the tops of the windows showed over the hedge" (110). Though,
as Alex explains to the narrator, the hedge keeps the wind out, it does not
prevent Johnny Bear from listening at windows. When Steinbeck's narrator is
curious, he peers in at the house "through one of the little wicket gates in the
cypress hedge" (115). Initially, any information he gets about the sisters comes
either second-hand through Alex Hartnell or by watching Johnny Bear's per-
formances. He finally sees them for the first and only time when they ride
to church. This experience solidifies his sense of the "monstrous" accuracy of
Johnny Bear's portrayal.

Another parallel is that the women, who are the subjects of these two
tales, although distant from their fellow townspeople, occupy vaunted posi-
tions in their societies. Faulkner's narrator begins by explaining that everyone
in the town went to Miss Emily's funeral out of "respectful affection for a
fallen monument" (119). At other points in his tale, the narrator refers to
her as "a tradition, a duty and a care" (119) and "an idol" (128). When she
is buried, her resting place is among the "august" names in the cemetery. In
"Johnny Bear" the unnamed narrator, who is new to the town, is told about
the Hawkins sisters by Alex Hartnell, a local farm owner. Hartnell explains,
"Every town has its aristocrats" and describes Emalin and Amy as Lomas'
"aristocrats, maiden ladies." Whereas it is hard to miss Faulkner's obvious
symbolism that equates Miss Emily with the old South, in Steinbeck's tale,
lest the reader miss the significance of the Hawkins sisters' position, it is made
explicit. Hartnell explains to the narrator: "These Hawkins women, they're
symbols . . ." (109). Additionally, their status derives from their father, who
was a congressman. Another parallel, although not of major significance, is
that the women in both stories use horse and buggy as means of conveyance.
Miss Emily rides with Homer Barron in a yellow-wheeled buggy drawn by a
matched team of bays. The Hawkins sisters appear in a shiny buggy, inscribed
with a big silver H on the outside of each blinder. An old, but well-groomed,
grey horse draws the buggy. Both authors utilize the horse and buggy image
to underline the chasm between the women, as symbols of the past, and a
current generation for which they serve as icons. In Steinbeck's story, the
sisters are in a buggy although the narrator and Hartnell are in a Model T
Ford. This further calls attention to their status as holdovers from a different
era. Although, Miss Emily's buggy rides occur in a time when there were
no automobiles, Faulkner emphasizes Miss Emily's association with bygone
times in his description of the garages and gasoline pumps that are part of the

scene at the beginning of the story, rendered in juxtaposition to the decay of what had once been the fashionable neighborhood where the Griersons lived.

An additional crucial similarity in both stories is that though the women have achieved iconic stature in their respective hometowns, as the plots unfold it is made clear that the reality of these women is at odds with their images. In fact, that distance between perception and reality is a key theme in both stories. In Faulkner's story, Miss Emily is initially pitied. The narrator recalls all the young men that her father had driven away, all of the young men who were "not quite good enough." Then the town fancies that she has been abandoned by Homer Barron and left to live alone in genteel poverty, only to find out, once she is safely buried, that this icon of Southern gentility and womanhood is most likely a murderer and a necrophile. In Steinbeck's story, the town comes to learn that Amy Hawkins, who has had a relationship with a Chinese sharecropper, is pregnant and has committed suicide. There is also a hint that perhaps her sister bears some responsibility in her death. Rather than understanding or supporting Amy, Emalin Hawkins tells her she'd be better off dead (108). This leads to the first suicide attempt. When the doctor comes the second time, too late to revive Amy, he accusingly remarks to Emalin that perhaps the knowledge of her sister's pregnancy is "why you didn't find her for so long" (118).

Still, both authors exhibit a certain amount of sympathy toward these women who are victims of a small-minded and rigid social structure. In this they are both presenting a muted critique of both the classicist and racist white male hegemony that governed the mores of the small towns they were brought up in. These views at once limit and venerate white womanhood. Both Miss Emily and Miss Amy are involved with men who are not considered appropriate for women of their station. "Of course a Grierson would not think seriously of a Northerner, a day laborer" (124) is the community consensus. Amy Hawkins's involvement with a Chinese laborer is not that explicit in the text. The reader must put the pieces of the puzzle together from Johnny Bear's presentations. Community horror at such a relationship can be inferred. Hartnell, the narrator's chief informant, uses the term "Chink" to define the sharecroppers that live on the Hawkins land. Both race and class would have been considered impediments to an appropriate relationship in the California of that time.

Another parallel is in the terminology each author uses to categorize the subjects of their stories. Both choose language that makes clear the iconic status of the women, the fact that these women are not just individuals but representative of their class. Faulkner's text refers to Miss Emily as a "fallen monument." In another instance she is described as looking like a "strained flag." In his choice of terms to describe the position the Hawkins sisters inhabit in their community, Steinbeck uses near synonymous language. After the men hear of the suicide of Miss Amy and the circumstances that led to it, the text reads: "They looked bewildered, for a *system* had fallen" (110–19; emphasis added).

As close as the stories are in setting, theme, and narrative stance, there is no evidence that Steinbeck was influenced by Faulkner's story. Both writers often wrote of stifling small town mores, of aberrant behavior and abnormal characters. Had Steinbeck read Faulkner's story of communal disillusionment when it is found that a representative of their sacred past is a "monster" to use Steinbeck's word? In the remembrance of Toby Street, the germ for Steinbeck's story was a very large mute man they encountered in a Bar just outside Castroville (Benson, 287). Rather than signing to communicate, the man clumsily illustrated or acted out what he did. At the time, Steinbeck commented to Street that a man like that could do a lot of harm. Therefore, it appears that Steinbeck was inspired by an actual character rather than one he read about in Faulkner.

His notes prior to beginning the story clue another source for Steinbeck. In those notes he refers to the story as "the sisters," a reference to gossip about two Salinas women, one who had had an affair with an Oriental man according to local gossip. Faulkner's story may also have been inspired by local gossip. Floyd C. Watkins theorized that the Miss Emily/Homer Barron story, at least initially, could have been derived from the marriage of Miss Mary Louis Neilson and Captain Jack Hume, an Oxford couple. Hume was a Yankee, with a colorful vocabulary who, against community and family objections, married a town aristocrat. Like Homer Barron, he had come to work on paving the streets of Oxford. Faulkner's story may be a projection of what might have happened if Miss Mary's love for Jack Hume had been frustrated. Thus it appears that both authors used sources close at hand from which to create their stories.

Later, when he was a more established writer, Steinbeck had, after seeing a Tennessee Williams play, referred to Williams and Faulkner as "the neurosis belt of the South." His remark was an obvious allusion to the fact that both writers emphasized the underside of humanity, predominantly decadence and deviation. In this comment, he seems unaware that critics had often called attention to the same traits in his writing. Steinbeck could easily have staked out his own little "neurosis belt of the West."

In the second set of stories, "Dry September" and "The Vigilante," Steinbeck and Faulkner both explore the dynamics of mob mentality and its psychosexual component, each story ending in a scene of post-coitallike tristesse. In both stories, a black man is lynched. Both stories incorporate oblique critiques of racism, the use of the black man as scapegoat. Nevertheless, while the themes are parallel, the path each author takes to that conclusion is markedly different. Both authors condemn the actions portrayed. Faulkner's denunciation is stronger than Steinbeck's because it is clear that an innocent man is murdered by a mob that has its own reasons for the lynching, many not having anything to do with the supposed crime.

Faulkner's story begins with a rumor, only vaguely identified as something about Miss Minnie and a Negro. The narrator makes it clear that no one sitting in the barbershop where the lynching is initiated "knew exactly what had happened" (169). In Steinbeck's story there is a more tangible basis for the mob execution. The man who is lynched is in jail, either accused or convicted of a crime. The text does not make that clear. The protagonist, Mike, says: "The papers all said he was a fiend. I read all the papers. That's what they all said" (98). The obvious innocence of Will Mayes makes Faulkner's story all the more powerful and a stronger denunciation of the lynch-mentality of his fellow Southerners. Steinbeck, for his part, includes dialog that calls into question the attitude toward black people that undergirds lynch-mentality. Welch, the bartender, inserts the comment: "I've known some pretty nice niggers" (98) and Mike agrees, "Well, I've knew some dam' fine niggers myself. I've worked right 'longside some niggers and they was as nice as any white man you could want to meet," but then to rationalize his participation in the lynching, he adds, "But not no fiends" (98).

In "Dry September" the plot proceeds through the incitement to violence and creation of the lynch mob, follows the group of men as they grab Will Mayes, but does not present the actual lynching. The reader leaves the scene on the way to the lynching when Hawkshaw, who cannot reason with the men, jumps out of the car. Steinbeck's story actually begins after the lynching. He presents graphic details that increase the horror of the reader. The "grey naked body" is hanging from an elm tree and members of the mob, not satisfied to have killed the man, are trying to burn him also. Thus it is clear that both authors are interested in the community mentality that countenances such brutality and in the way the individual is affected, rather than in portraying the actual violence and horror of the lynching itself.

In structuring plot lines as they unveil their similar critiques of the inspiration for and results of violence, each author chooses to come at his story quite differently. Faulkner's focus is diffuse. Three stories are unfolded: that of the incitement to violence and the frustration and ineffectuality of one man (Hawkshaw), trying to stop the mob on the one hand and the story of Miss Minnie Cooper, an aging spinster who is no longer the object of male attention. The third story is that of McClendon, the man who incites the mob. Though Hawkshaw is generally read as exemplifying the reasonable southerner, one who stands up for Will Mayes and tries to get the men to investigate the facts before they act, Karen Andrews finds his story evidence of Faulkner's "multilayered critique of the miscegenation/rape complex" and only a "counterhegemonic voice" on the most obvious level (497). She argues that his character is Faulkner's more subtle critique of white paternalism. Hawkshaw's plot line ends when he jumps out of the car speeding to the lynching of Will Mayes and is left retching in a ditch along the country road.

The plot then picks up the story of Miss Minnie Cooper, whose complicity in this murder is suggested by her advancing years, sexual frustration, and need for attention. Whereas it has been her fate that the "sitting and lounging men did not even follow her with their eyes any more" (175) she is returned to a subject of interest after this supposed incident when "their eyes [followed] the motion of her hips and legs when she passed" (181). Minnie's story concludes with her hysterical laughter and her friends' "eyes darkly aglitter, secret and passionate" (182) questioning whether anything really had happened. The final plot spotlight is on McLendon, the leader of the mob, returning home.

Steinbeck's plot is more linear. His focus is on a single individual, Mike, and on his reactions, physical and emotional, to having participated in a lynching. Steinbeck does not provide his protagonist with a last name, thus reinforcing the sense that he may be representative of a type. Faulkner's characters, particularly Miss Minnie Cooper, have histories. The reader knows some of their back stories, a necessity for Faulkner's theme of how the black man serves as a scapegoat for everything from weather (Dry September) to marital discord. Steinbeck gives us only the actions of one night. After the lynching, everything has fallen to silence. Mike feels the "letdown." He remembers "howling with the mob and fighting for a chance to help to pull the rope" (94), but now experiences the "unreality." There are physical aftermaths also; his chest hurts as he had been crushed against the door of the jail. Steinbeck does not glamorize the violence or its effect. "A cold loneliness" encompasses Mike once he is no longer part of the mob. Mike wants to believe in the significance of what he has done, but though "his brain told him this was a terrible and important affair" (94), what Mike sees and what he feels contradict his thoughts. He sees it as "ordinary." His sin, like that of the Ancient Mariner, requires that he tell his story. He goes into a bar and tells his tale to the mousy bartender, Welch, a newcomer to town. In an attempt to rationalize his actions, Mike argues: "There's times when citizens got to take the law in their own hands. Sneaky lawyer comes along and gets some fiend out of it" (95).

At the end of "The Vigilante" Mike goes home to his "thin, petulant wife." She accuses him of infidelity, "What woman you been with?" The basis for her accusation is the look on his face. The story ends with his looking in the mirror and realizing why she thought he had just had sex. "By God, she was right," he thought. "That's just exactly how I do feel." Steinbeck also reinforces the parallel between the aftermaths of sex and violence in his description of how Mike responds to Welch's question of how participating in the lynching made him feel. Mike uses the words, "tired" and "satisfied," concluding "Like you done a good job—but tired and kind of sleepy" (99).

The final scene of "Dry September" presents a similar picture. McClendon, the war veteran who is the putative leader of the lynching, returns to his "neat, new house." His wife's face is described as "pale, strained, and weary-looking." The idea that she may be concerned about his fidelity is suggested by his lines: "Haven't I told you about sitting up like this, waiting to see when I come in?" In Faulkner's text there is the suggestion that McClendon's sexual energies have not been expended in the violence of the lynching. His abuse of his wife, half striking and half flinging her across a chair, indicates an abiding brutality. In both stories there is the suggestion that failed marital relationships contribute to the violent behaviors of these men, that the satisfaction of violence substitutes for sexual satisfaction.

While the first two stories demonstrate how both Steinbeck and Faulkner were sensitive to the harmful effects of sublimated female sexuality and of small-town prejudices, the second two are examples of their avant-garde attitudes toward the bigotry and prejudices of their communities, the abhorrence for lynch mob justice. Of course, there are many other layers to these four intriguing stories.

There are many factors that may have contributed to the resonance between the works of these two giants of American literature. In his study of Faulkner's short fiction, James B. Carothers notes that Faulkner believed that "a book of short stories should be lined together by characters or chronology" (58). That Steinbeck had similar views is demonstrated by his short stories cycles. In *The Pastures of Heaven* the stories are linked not only by character, but also by setting. While setting mostly links the stories in *The Long Valley*, the Red Pony stories and "A Leader of the People" are linked by character. As Faulkner's stories were published first, one might conjecture that Steinbeck was influenced by the older writer, but there is no evidence that Steinbeck had read Faulkner's stories when he wrote his. Steinbeck's library did contain a number of Faulkner volumes, but not *These 13*. He did own a copy of *Collected Stories*, but that was a late acquisition, not having been published until 1950.

There are a number of fine studies in which the various works of Hemingway and Steinbeck are compared. Steinbeck once observed that in the early part of his career he tried to write like Hemingway. Comparisons of Steinbeck and Faulkner, however, are rarely made. That is regrettable as there are some interesting connections. In 1948 both men were elected to membership in the American Academy of Arts and Letters. After their disastrous first meeting, the two men did establish a warmer relationship. Faulkner apologized for his behavior. The two men did not like to talk about their writing, but they found their common interests in hunting, fishing, dogs, and horses good ground for an amiable association. In 1956, Steinbeck responded to Faulkner's call to join the writer's committee of the "People to People Program." Their participation there was amicable. When Faulkner was asked to rate his contemporaries as to their writing skills, including himself, Steinbeck was in his top five. Surrounded by reporters upon receiving notice of his Nobel Prize, Steinbeck was asked to name his favorite authors. "Faulkner and Hemingway" was his immediate response. This he qualified by explaining that he meant Hemingway's short stories and nearly everything Faulkner wrote. Though there is no evidence of direct influence in either man's works of the writings of the other, their mutual admiration may be what accounts for the resonance found in the early short stories of these two giants of American literature.

Notes

1. All page references are from *The Long Valley* (New York: Penguin Books, 1938).

2. All page references are from *Collected Stories of William Faulkner* (New York: Random House, 1950).

STEPHEN K. GEORGE

"Surrendering to the Feminine": Implied Author Compassion in "The Chrysanthemums" and "Hills Like White Elephants"

As a senior at Brigham Young University in winter of 1990, I took a course in American Modernism from a provocative feminist professor with definite ideas concerning Ernest Hemingway's literary depictions of women. I remember writing a short critical response to *For Whom the Bell Tolls* in which I argued that Hemingway's depiction of Maria, his "little rabbit" (159), was not necessarily sexist because, in my view, such emotionally dependent and subservient women actually existed in the real world and that, given Maria's history of abuse, such a portrayal was psychologically valid. My professor, a fine critic and theorist, did not agree. The "B" from that paper still leaves a bad taste in my mouth, mostly because my interpretation seemed dismissed out of hand by my professor's insistence on seeing Hemingway, as well as peers such as John Steinbeck and F. Scott Fitzgerald, as incapable of fully portraying or realizing women in literary form.

Such limitations surrounding Steinbeck's and Hemingway's depictions of female characters have been engrained into the mindsets of college professors and students for decades now. These stereotypes include the following:

1. Both of these dead, white, male Nobel Laureates were constrained by their social circumstances to see women in very limited, often sexist roles. These views were then translated, consciously or subconsciously, into the depictions of their female characters.

From *John Steinbeck and His Contemporaries*, edited by Stephen K. George and Barbara A. Heavilin, pp. 61–67. Copyright © 2007 by Stephen K. George and Barbara A. Heavilin.

2. Both writers have a paucity of strong, female characters in their works. There are exceptions of course—Ma Joad, Brett Ashley, Juana from *The Pearl*, Pilar from *For Whom the Bell Tolls*—but largely these authors write from a man's perspective. Steinbeck's feminine world ranges from whores to housewives; Hemingway's from male sufficiency to stoic independence.

3. Steinbeck and Hemingway personally had difficulty relating to women, as evident in part by their many failed marriages, which difficulty translates into their limited female characterizations. As biographers Carlos Baker and Jay Parini confirm, the authors were often incredibly insensitive to and dismissive of the strong women in their lives, including their wives.[1]

Although all of these views have some substance of truth, such stereotypes are now being directly challenged by scholarship aimed at reevaluating these two writers' sensitivities in portraying the feminine in literature. One particularly impressive study is the recent critical collection *Hemingway and Women: Female Critics and the Female Voice*, with seventeen essays re-examining the complex relations among the author, his female characters, and the real women in his life. An overarching argument of the book is that gender and male-female relations were a "constant concern" in Hemingway's work from beginning to end, with "his female characters . . . drawn with [a] complexity and individuality equal to Hemingway's males" (Broer and Holland xi). Critic Ann Putnam then goes further to argue that Ernest Hemingway, throughout his career, was especially sensitive to the limitations of "male language" in contrast to the intricacies and meaningful silences of "female language," a sensitivity shown most "clearly . . . in such lyric short stories as 'Hills Like White Elephants' and 'Cat in the Rain'" (123). Nancy Comley continues by concluding, after an in-depth analysis of Hemingway's *The Garden of Eden*, that this manuscript "introduces the woman reader to a more complex, more interesting Hemingway, one who plays and questions the masculine role" (217). Finally, critic Lisa Tyler, who focuses on male/female discourse in two of the author's short stories, concludes that Hemingway's "dissections of the sexual politics of heterosexual relationships are dazzling in their precision and accuracy," so much so that "his critics [may] have all too often read them in ways that reveal the fault lines in their own sexual politics" (80). Clearly critical tides are changing within the Hemingway world concerning the issue of the author's literary sensitivity to the other sex.

Leading the way in a reevaluation of John Steinbeck's literary depictions of the feminine is critic Mimi Gladstein, the pioneer of feminist interpretations of Steinbeck. In her 2002 essay, "Steinbeck and the Woman Question: A Never Ending Puzzle," she acknowledges both the past parameters of reading the author (Steinbeck's lack of acknowledging the powerful and intelligent women in his life, the male-dominated literary worlds of his 1930s works),

yet she remains puzzled at the strong women—Ma Joad, Abra Trask, Juana—
that fill essential roles in Steinbeck's major novels (108–109). In "Masculine
Sexuality and the Objectification of the Female," Gladstein compares the bla-
tant objectification of women as commodities in *Cannery Row* to Steinbeck's
sensitive portrayal of Camille Oaks fending off male sexual aggression in *The
Wayward Bus*. Gladstein, while noting that the author was sympathetic to the
objectification of Curley's wife in the 1937 *Of Mice and Men*, suggests that
Steinbeck may have waited until the 1947 *Wayward Bus* to more fully explore
the female psyche because he did not feel comfortable or qualified until then
"to enter into the feminine mind" (120). In other words, the John Steinbeck
of the 1930s was not experienced or talented enough to sensitively portray
the feminine in his work.

Although this debate will undoubtedly continue to puzzle critics, I would
argue that the sensitivities to the feminine of these two authors are evident
much earlier in their careers, most strikingly in Steinbeck's 1934 story "The
Chrysanthemums" and Hemingway's 1927 "Hills Like White Elephants."
The uncanny parallels between these stories include how the authors char-
acterized their protagonists, Elisa Allen and Jig; how deftly the settings of
these stories complement these characterizations and foreshadow the major
conflicts each woman faces; and how the male antagonists, the pot mender
and the American, subtly use manipulative language and false sympathy to
get what they want. Moreover, by applying the concept of "implied author,"
as propounded by ethical critics such as Wayne Booth, to these stories, we can
see how such conscious decisions of characterization, setting, and conflict all
direct the reader to a much more sensitive view of Hemingway and Steinbeck
in characterizing the other sex. Rather than a wall of gender blindness, an
undeniable compassion for Elisa Allen's and Jig's situations flows from the
artistic choices of these authors.

The concept of the "implied author" is most clearly stated in Wayne
Booth's seminal work, *The Company We Keep: An Ethics of Fiction*. In response
to some postmodernists' insistence that an author's intentions or values have
no relevance to her audience and that texts exist as entities apart from the real
world, Booth sought to clarify the ethical responsibilities artists and writers have for what they create—for the moral impact of their ideas, world
views, and creative choices upon their readers. He does this by dividing the
traditional notion of "author" into three authorial presences: the "narrator"
or "immediate teller" of a story (such as Huck Finn), the "implied author"
(Mark Twain) whose presence informs the choices made during the creation
of the text and "who takes responsibility for" such choices, and the "flesh-
and-blood" author (Samuel Clemens) whose life goes on after the creation
of the text (125). As Booth argues in "Why Ethical Criticism Can Never Be

Simple," the author-is-dead-crowd does not distinguish between the flesh-and-blood author, for whom the creation of a work is one part of his career "and the actualized text's intentions: what one can infer from the collection of choices that every work worth bothering about reveals" (28). It is in analyzing the artistic choices of the "implied author" that the moral values and world view of a particular story surfaces. Indeed, Booth concludes, "I can think of no published story that does not exhibit its author's implied judgments about how to live and what to believe about how to live" (26).

The artistic choices made by the implied authors of "The Chrysanthemums" and "Hills Like White Elephants" in developing Elisa Allen and Jig reveal how much Steinbeck and Hemingway sympathized with the dreams and unfulfilled needs of these characters. The two women do share significant differences. Elisa is married, mature, a farm wife who longs to travel and experience the outside world. Jig is (we assume) single and living with her American companion, younger than Elisa, and, as evidenced from the hotel labels on their luggage, living the very lifestyle that Elisa dreams of. But the similarities of their situations are also clear. Neither is really satisfied with the direction of their lives, with Jig desiring a stable family relationship where she and her partner "can [truly] have everything" (1424) and Elisa wishing for a life of variety, growth, and self-expression—what she describes to the pot mender as "a nice kind of way to live" (5). The focus in the stories on the longings of these women, in contrast to the satisfied and assured situations of Elisa's husband Henry and Jig's American companion, highlights the intent of these stories for the audience to sympathize with Elisa and Jig's lack of fulfillment and general despair.

This sympathy is further reinforced by how the stories' settings emphasize the oppressive circumstances of the women and foreshadow the conflicts to come. As most critics admit, John Steinbeck and Ernest Hemingway were masters of creating a time, place, and context that powerfully admitted the reader into their literary worlds. Both stories begin with such descriptions. "Hills Like White Elephants" begins, "The hills across the valley of the Ebro were long and white. On this side there was no shade and no trees and the station was between two lines of rails in the sun. . . . The American and the girl with him sat at a table in the shade, outside the building" (1,422). Later, in the midst of their struggle over whether the *girl* should have the abortion the *man* is encouraging, Jig stands and looks across the valley: "Across, on the other side, were fields of grain and trees along the banks of the Ebro. Far away, beyond the river, were mountains. The shadow of a cloud moved across the field of grain and she saw the river through the trees. 'And we could have all of this,' she said" (14–24).

In "The Chrysanthemums," Elisa Allen's own repressive circumstances are foreshadowed in the story's first lines:

The high grey-flannel fog of winter closed off the Salinas Valley
from the sky and from all the rest of the world. On every side it sat
like a lid on the mountains and made of the great valley a closed
pot. On the broad, level land floor the gang plows bit deep and left
the black earth shining like metal where the shares had cut. . . .
[T]here was no sunshine in the valley now in December. . . . It was
a time of quiet and waiting. (1)

Again, an opening description that emphasizes the repressive, "closed off"
confines of Elisa's life, a season without "sunshine" but rather "quiet and
waiting" (1).

In choosing to begin both stories with such descriptions, the implied
authors immediately draw their audience to the unfulfilled, circumscribed
situations of the female protagonists. As critics and readers have consistently
noted, Jig's choice of a future with husband and child versus their continued
globetrotting of Europe is symbolically represented in the depiction of the
Ebro valley, with its barren landscape without shade or tree on one hand and
the "field of grain" and "river through the trees" on the other. Jig longs for
the future offered by the fertile side of the valley; as she concludes, "'And we
could have everything and every day we make it more impossible'" (1,424).
Likewise, Elisa Allen's desire to determine for herself what kind of life a
woman should have—as shown in her challenge to the pot mender's "'It ain't
the right kind of life for a woman'" with "'How can you tell?'" (9)—is contex-
tually constrained within a "great valley" that is closed off "from the sky and
the rest of the world" (1). Both settings reinforce the narrow range of choices
available to these two women while also preparing the reader for the conflicts
to come.

The strongest evidence for implied author sympathy for Jig and Elisa
rests with the male-female conflicts within the stories and how unsympathet-
ically the male antagonists are drawn by the authors. In "Hills Like White
Elephants," the hierarchy of power is clear: the mature American "man," clear
headed and rational, who tells Jig, "'You mustn't feel that way,'" versus the
intuitive, emotional "girl" who "just knows things" (1,424). The vulnerability
of Jig's situation—pregnant, presumably unwed, financially dependent—is
made even more poignant by her self-disparaging remarks, "'Then I'll do it
[have the abortion]. Because I don't care about me,'" and final denial at the
story's end of both self and her desire for a child and family: "'I feel fine,' she
said. 'There's nothing wrong with me. I feel fine'" (1,425).

In contrast, the false sympathy and subtle manipulation of her companion—rendered powerfully from Hemingway's third person objective point of
view—reveal a man who doesn't want to take responsibility for Jig's pregnancy

and who selfishly wishes for their life of drink, travel, hotel-hopping, and consequence-free sex to continue. His assertion that "'It's really an awfully simple operation. . . . not really an operation at all . . .' (1,423) rings untrue—exactly how would he know this for certain? Likewise, his overwrought insistence that he doesn't want Jig to do anything she doesn't want to, that he's willing to have the child "'if it means anything to . . . the girl (which obviously it does),'" that he would "'do anything for . . . her'" (1,424), reveal a man who knows the power of pretended sympathy in manipulating his emotionally distraught and vulnerable companion.

The manipulation of Elisa Allen by the pot mender in "The Chrysanthemums" is no less disturbing. A master at knowing how to ply his trade as he follows his annual circuit from San Diego to Seattle, he first attempts humor to open Elisa up, yet it's a mirth that disappears "from his face and eyes the moment his laughing voice ceased" (4–5), "an empty laugh" mirroring his empty sympathy (Gorton 94). He next tries the common sales technique of asking for help with directions to soften her with his plight, and then resorts to outright pleading: "'I ain't had a thing to do today. Maybe I won't have no supper tonight.'" To this Elisa firmly responds, "'I haven't anything for you to do'" (6). Yet this is no ordinary peddler. Noticing Elisa's loving care over her budding chrysanthemums, the pot mender transforms from a greasy, "stubble-bearded man" to a poet, describing the chrysanthemums as "'[k]ind of a long-stemmed flower . . . like a quick puff of colored smoke,'" to which Elisa responds, "'That's it. What a nice way to describe them'" (4, 6).

From this point on in the story, Elisa is, to a degree, at the mercy of the pot mender, who has found the key to what he wants—fifty cents for fixing two saucepans and the pot carrying seedlings to the non-existent "lady down the road apiece" (6)—by exploiting Elisa's passion for her flowers, a passion directly linked to her longing for a life of meaning beyond her confined existence on their foothill ranch. At Elisa's moment of greatest vulnerability, as she kneels before the pot mender and confides her own lonely nights where "'the stars are sharp-pointed, and there's quiet,'" and "'Every pointed star gets driven into your body. . . . Hot and sharp and—lovely,'" the peddler springs his trap: "'It's nice, just like you say. Only when you don't have no dinner, it ain't'" (8). Unlike the American in Hemingway's story, whose culpability concerning Jig and the pressured abortion is of far greater moral significance, the pot mender's manipulations are reprehensible but pragmatically understandable—he dumps the seedlings on the road because "He had to keep the pot" (12). Yet Elisa's grief and complete vulnerability, her realization that her opening of her innermost self to this stranger was a purely one-way exchange, is profoundly disturbing to the story's audience. And this, I am sure, is what the implied author of "The Chrysanthemums" intended.

In Valerie Hemingway's 2004 biography, *Running with the Bulls: My Years with the Hemingways*, she tells the story of a friend of Hemingway's, business man Lee Samuels, who had never discovered a book written by a woman that was worth reading. Hemingway offered his friend works by several of his favorite female writers, including Isak Dinesen and Dawn Powell, but to no avail. Later he lent Samuels *The Reason Why*, by Cecil Woodham-Smith, which Samuels thoroughly enjoyed. Months later, after his friend had continued to offer effusive praise over the book, Ernest innocently asked:

> "You enjoyed *The Reason Why*?"
> "But of course."
> "And Cecil Woodham-Smith is a writer you have no trouble reading."
> "Certainly not."
> "And since she is a woman. . . ." (105)

According to Ms. Hemingway, this was one of Hemingway's favorite stories, "pointing to the fallibility of self-styled literary experts" (105). But more importantly, from my perspective it shows the professional respect that Ernest Hemingway had for any writer of ability, a trait likewise shared by John Steinbeck.[2]

The sensitivity with which the female protagonists of "Hills Like White Elephants" and "The Chrysanthemums" are portrayed, the careful renderings of setting to mirror their oppressive circumstances, the detailed depictions of male manipulations—all indicate deliberate choices by implied authors motivated, first and foremost, by a compassion for these two female characters and for women generally in such circumstances. Admittedly, the flesh-and-blood authors were not so easily defined; as Gladstein writes of Steinbeck, some who knew him closest found a man who "had problems relating women" while others "found him quite gallant and responsive" ("Steinbeck" 112). Yet as Wayne Booth argues, implied authors, through the process of harmonizing competing textual intentions, almost always represent the flesh-and-blood author's best self ("Why" 29). And it is this best self that comes through in the stories, a self that shows "Hemingway's women, more often than his men, . . . [as understanding and confronting] the complexities of life and of male/female relationships" (Miller 10), and of Steinbeck calling "into question and . . . [challenging] simplistic notions of gender roles . . . [and] the 'limitations of femininity'" (Gorton 90). Indeed, Lorelei Cederstrom argues that "[a]bove all, Steinbeck's novels reveal his deep respect for the balance between the masculine and feminine upon which not only every man/woman relationship but also the health of the earth itself depends" (204), a balance also explored and defended by Hemingway. As these two early stories make clear, Ernest Hemingway and John Steinbeck indeed surrender to the feminine in their empathetic portrayals of Jig and Elisa Allen.

NOTES

1. Steinbeck's and Hemingway's relationships with women were both complex and contradictory, as evidenced by their cumulative seven marriages (Steinbeck to Carol Henning, Gwyn Conger, and Elaine Scott; Hemingway to Hadley Richardson, Pauline Pfeiffer, Martha Gellhorn, and Mary Welsh). For example, according to Jay Parini and Carlos Baker, both men regretted to the end their treatment of their first wives, Carol and Hadley, who played such major roles in their careers. According to Baker, Hemingway blamed himself "for the breakup of all his marriages except the one to Martha [Gellhorn]" (452). On Steinbeck's part (and in eerie connection to "Hills Like White Elephants"), he deeply regretted having insisted on Carol getting an abortion, which operation led to an infection and "complete hysterectomy," leaving her unable to have children (Parini 227). Both authors, while extremely difficult to live with, were aware of their own shortcomings and the pain they caused to the women in their lives.

2. Arguably, the most important people in Steinbeck's writing career were women: Professor Margery Bailey, who marked the budding author as a "protégé"; Edith Mirrielees, the "short-story teacher [who] . . . had the most profound effect upon him of all his Stanford professors"; and Elizabeth Otis, the literary agent who represented Steinbeck for nearly forty years and was perhaps the most influential person in his writing (Benson 55, 58, 213). And as with Hemingway's open admiration of female writers Isak Dinesen and Dawn Powell, Steinbeck openly applauded the work of George Eliot (whose writing was "realer than experience"), Katherine Fullerton Gerould (a "master of her kind of short stories"), and Rebecca West (Benson 23, 78).

CHARLOTTE COOK HADELLA

Lonely Ladies and Landscapes: A Comparison of John Steinbeck's "The White Quail" and Eudora Welty's "A Curtain of Green"

From the beginning of her literary career to the end, Eudora Welty concerned herself with the status and images of women in small-town America while avoiding the abrasive discourse against the patriarchy which often accompanies feminist critiques of such communities. Nevertheless, Welty did not overlook the gender-specific difficulties for women in rural society. Likewise, John Steinbeck, particularly in his early short stories, also featured women such as Elisa Allen in "The Chrysanthemums," Jelka in "The Murder," and Amy Hawkins in "Johnny Bear" who seek personal fulfillment beyond the boundaries of their sanctioned spheres. In early story collections by each author—Steinbeck's *The Long Valley*, published in 1938, and Welty's *A Curtain of Green*, published in 1941—a number of female characters are lonely, repressed, and in some cases depraved because of the patriarchal forces which mold their personalities and limit their arenas of action.[1]

In these story collections, appearing within a few years of each other, we encounter women who are unfulfilled in their roles as housewives—Elisa Allen in Steinbeck's "The Chrysanthemums" and Livvi in Welty's story "Livvi," for example. Yet the conflict resolution for these two stories reveals obvious contrasts: Elisa cries "weakly—like an old woman" (Steinbeck 18), while Livvi dances into the "bursting light of spring" (Welty 239). Stories about marital infidelity highlight similar contrasts: Jelka, in Steinbeck's "The

Murder," conforms to obedient servitude after being beaten by her husband, while Ruby Fisher, in Welty's "A Piece of News," never admits her indiscretions. As Peter Schmidt points out in *The Heart of the Story*, Ruby's husband, Clyde, "refuses to act out the role of the conventional angry husband. Instead, he parodies it in a way that seems to be his unarticulated recognition of Ruby's right to have a double life not defined solely by her marriage to him" (36). In this story and others, Welty emphasizes the power of women to transcend socially constructed norms.

Although Steinbeck resisted the oversimplification of the cause/effect relationship between unfulfilled womanhood and the power of the patriarchy, his exploration of this theme generally blames patriarchal constructs of idealized womanhood for limiting and entrapping women. His short story "The White Quail," the subject of extensive critical commentary, crystallizes Steinbeck's treatment of this theme (Hadella 65–69). On the other hand, instead of pointing fingers, laying blame, so to speak, Welty weaves a complex system of symbols and imagery to illustrate how both men and women often conspire unconsciously to coerce a female member of the community into conformity. In "A Curtain of Green," the title story of Welty's first anthology (originally published in the *Southern Review* in 1939), a woman's garden clearly symbolizes both sociological and psychological entrapment. Welty, however, complicates the symbology, turning the garden imagery back upon itself, until it evolves into a mechanism for personal expression, rebellion, and release rather than conformity and confinement. This impulse to push the garden metaphor beyond either a replication or a refutation of the Eden myth as it is employed by Steinbeck (Owens 100) characterizes a key difference between Steinbeck's depiction of women in early to mid-twentieth century America and Welty's representation of women during that same time period. Close readings of "The White Quail" and "A Curtain of Green" bring this contrast into sharp focus.

From an omniscient narrative voice, the opening of "The White Quail" establishes the garden as a central symbol of the story. By the end of paragraph three, the narrative voice has fused with Mary Teller's voice and the controlling image of the garden has fused with Mary as well. In a mock dialectical questioning of herself about finding a husband, Mary says, "She didn't think so much, 'Would this man like such a garden?' but, 'Would the garden like such a man?' For the garden was herself, and after all she had to marry some one she liked" (22).

That Mary likes her prospective husband is not positively established in the first section of the story, however. The fourth paragraph begins with "When she met Harry Teller, the garden seemed to like him" (22). And then she remembers that she "let him kiss her," but when he became too ardent and expressed his lust with "You make me kind of hungry" (and one naturally goes to a garden for food when hungry), she became annoyed and "sent him home" (23). Mary's confusion about the nature of commitment that marriage requires is evident from the beginning of the story. Her only concept of commitment is of her commitment to herself as an individual apart from everyone and everything. At one with her perfect, sterile garden, Mary is unable to participate in a union with another person. Marriage is simply a means to an end for her, and that end is total isolation.

Thus Steinbeck presents Mary Teller in "The White Quail" as a woman whose perceptions are warped. Marilyn Mitchell, commenting on the opening paragraphs of the story, notes: "Steinbeck introduces the reader to the narrow world of Mary Teller's garden through a dormer window composed of leaded, diamond-shaped panes. The convex curvature of the window and the fragmentation of its space indicate that the vision of the person within, Mary Teller, is distorted" (28). Later in the story, Steinbeck employs this same technique to emphasize Mary's distorted perception of her marriage by reversing her position and having her outside in her garden looking into her living room and imagining that she sees herself sitting there with her husband. The scene, to her, is "like a picture, like a set of a play that was about to start" (27).

A number of critics have concluded that Mary's perceptions are warped and she is only deceiving herself to think that she will create something that "won't ever change" (24), whether it be a garden or a marriage. Louis Owens views Mary's garden "as a barrier between herself and all contact with the world outside . . . an attempt to construct an unfallen Eden in a fallen world, a neurotic projection of Mary's self" (113). Arthur Simpson, in discussing Mary's garden as a form of artistic withdrawal, says that it represents "static perfection" (12). And Brian Barbour comments that although a garden basically symbolizes fertility, Steinbeck uses it ironically "to deny change . . . and as a manifestation of Mary's sexual inhibition. . . . She keeps her garden, as she keeps herself, untrammeled" (117).

Yet Steinbeck does not hold Mary totally responsible for the sterile, static condition of her life and her marriage. In Part II of "The White Quail," Harry becomes a willing partner in the illusive quest for a perfect Eden, a quest that destroys the couple's chances for a rewarding relationship. His admiration as she supervises the creation of the garden pleases Mary so much that she extends the following invitation: "You can plant some of the things you like in the garden, if you want" (23). Harry declines immediately what, in the context of the story's symbolism, is his only opportunity to consummate the marriage. And Mary, of course, "loved him for that" (24). But once her garden is completed just the way she wants it, with no contributions from Harry except his awe, Mary expresses a moment of misgiving when she says, "in a way I'm sad that it's done," which is followed by, "But mostly I'm glad. We won't ever change it, will we Harry? If a bush dies, we'll put another one just like it in the same place" (24). Mary's appointment of Harry as a keeper of the perfect Eden indicates her perception of his willingness to preserve the garden, forever untouched, unchanged—in other words, his willingness to preserve her chastity.

Stanley Renner, who describes Mary Teller as "ethereal, unearthly, flesh-less," contends that the devotion she inspires from Harry is "suggestive of divine adoration rather than earthly love" ("Birds of a Feather" 37). Renner also acknowledges that Harry is a partner in Mary's self-idealization which is "set in the larger *cultural* idealization of womanhood itself" (36). Harry's comments at the end of Part II certainly support his role as worshipper of purity. He admits his fear of violating Mary (the garden) and he calls her "untouchable" (25). She responds with, "You let me do it. You made it my garden" (25). Renner observes that in "the pointless heart-shaped pool" which is the centerpiece of the garden, "Steinbeck has deftly symbolized the romantic ideal that lies at the heart of it all, a spiritualized, sexless, and thus, in several senses, pointless love" ("Sexual Idealism" 79).

Part II of the story features the description of the couple killing slugs and snails together in the garden, the introduction of the threatening cat, and Mary's speech proclaiming her fuchsias as a fortress from the "rough and tangle" world that wants to get into her garden (26). Critics agree that Harry's sexual needs are identified with the stalking cat which is mentioned in Part III, preparing the reader for the information in Part IV that Mary always locked her bedroom door and that Harry always tried the door silently" (30). Mary muses that it "seemed to make him ashamed when he turned the knob and found the door locked," but her response is to turn out the light in her bedroom and look out the window "at her garden in the half moonlight" (30). In this way, Steinbeck shows Mary retreating further into her unnatural world of illusory perception as Harry becomes less able to suppress his natural sexual urges.

Though Renner is correct in noting that the final two sections of the story "move toward a striking climax that dramatizes the explosive potential of the unconscious stresses building up in the marriage" ("Sexual Idealism" 83, 85), his contentions that Harry kills the quail unintentionally, and that this act shows Harry finally succumbing to his sexual urges in spite of Mary's protests, seem contradictory. It is more logical to assume that in a world as symbolically contrived as the world of the Teller's marriage, Steinbeck allows Harry to kill the white quail intentionally. Harry's violence against the symbol of Mary's chastity, an essence boiled down to utter purity (33), is a symbolic action by a character who is incapable of real action. It is also important to note that the cat does not even enter the picture in this scene. Mary's hysterical reaction may have scared him away from her garden forever; or Harry may simply have become the cat, symbolically.

Steinbeck includes a subtle detail in Part V of the story to underline Mary's ability to dominate Harry so thoroughly that he is only capable of symbolic violence. Just after she sees the white quail, Mary experiences a series of memories that she associates with the kind of pleasure that she felt at that moment. One of those memories is simply a statement someone once made about her—"She's like a gentian, so quite"—a statement which filled her with "an ecstasy" like the ecstasy in seeing the white quail (33). A gentian is a medicinal plant that destroys bacteria, and Mary, like a gentian, has sterilized her marriage completely, so completely that Harry is incapable of contaminating it even if he refuses to poison the cat.

The narrative shift from Mary's point of view to Harry's point of view at the end of the story emphasizes the total lack of understanding between man and wife. She cannot perceive of the despair that causes him to kill the quail. But the fact that the cat does not even appear in this scene indicates that Harry's violence against the quail and his remorse afterward are not simply eruptions of violent sexual urges but expressions of the altered environment of the marriage. Harry has become the cat, the Old Harry in Mary's Eden, the sexual threat, the potential "fall" that cannot be exorcised; but on a realistic level, he and Mary cannot interact as marriage partners unless he resorts to violence and forcefully invades her cloistral chamber.

Steinbeck suggests that self-induced isolation results from concepts of womanhood espoused by an American society which quests for an illusory Eden. He also demonstrates that such sterile self-repression affects not only the females, but inspires violent reactions from the men who attempt to interact with them. Harry never confronts Mary openly with his hostility; instead he deliberately kills the white quail that she begs him to rescue, and then he cries aloud to an empty room, "Oh, Lord, I'm so lonely!" (37). Although "The White Quail" does not present a particularly sympathetic view of the central female character, the story clearly implies that the disunity in the marriage can be blamed on male idealization of female perfection.

A sense of isolation and loneliness also dominates Welty's story "A Curtain of Green," but in this story, the wife longs for the male/female union. Unfortunately, such a union is impossible because the husband is deceased. Welty opens the story with this fact: Mrs. Larkin, since the day that her husband was killed by a falling chinaberry tree, has "never once been seen anywhere else" but her garden (107). Welty writes:

> Within its border of hedge, high like a wall, and visible only
> from the upstairs windows of the neighbors, this slanting, tangled

garden, more and more overabundant and confusing, must have become so familiar to Mrs. Larkin that quite possibly by now she was unable to conceive of any other place. (107)

The widow's link to humanity seems to have been severed with the death of her husband. Mr. Larkin, for whose father the town of Larkin's Hill had been named, had obviously been a respected citizen, and the townspeople had extended that respect to his wife as well. The women of the town, we are told, "had called upon the widow with decent frequency" (108). However, when Mrs. Larkin does not respond as they wish, they withdraw, leaving her alone, only thinking of her when they "looked down from their bedroom windows as they brushed studiously at their hair in the morning" (108). Stressing the extremity of the rift between Mrs. Larkin and the other women of Larkin's Hill, Welty notes that from their windows, "[t]hey found her place in the garden, as they might have run their fingers toward a city on a map of a foreign country, located her from their distance almost in curiosity, and then forgot her" (108). As Peter Schmidt points out, the world of the deceased husband "belongs to the front of the house, the world of Larkin's Hill, whereas the only area in which his wife can imagine living is *behind* the house, slanting away almost obscured from view on the 'other' or 'back' side of the hill on which the town is founded. Mrs. Larkin thus cultivates a secret life on the other side of the town's public space, a subversive doubling and disfiguring that expresses both energy and despair, entrapping her even as it provides a form of release" (26).

Mrs. Larkin has obviously rejected the traditional role reserved for her—the passive, seemingly trivial existence of her female neighbors who appear "in the windows of their houses, fanning and sighing, waiting for the rain" (107). On the day that the events of the story take place, as the women watch Mrs. Larkin,

> the intense light like a tweezers picked out her clumsy, small figure in its old pair of men's overalls rolled up at the sleeves and trousers, separated it from the thick leaves, and made it look strange and yellow as she worked with a hoe—over-vigorous, disreputable, and heedless. (107)

The extravagant recklessness of Mrs. Larkin's garden, in fact, is what separates her from the other women in the town whose lives are ordered by tree-lined streets, rows of flower gardens, and window frames. Rebelling against such monotony, "Mrs. Larkin rarely cut, separated, tied back [her plants]. . . . To a certain extent, she seemed not to seek for order, but to allow an over-flowering, as if she consciously ventured forever a little farther, a little deeper, into her life in the garden" (108). Welty also stresses details of appearance and behavior to emphasize that Mrs. Larkin is becoming more and more like her garden and less like other women of the town: her hair is "streaming and tangled"; she wanders about "uncertainly, deep among the plants and wet with their dew" (107).

Referring to Welty's use of landscape in *Losing Battles*, Lucinda MacKethan makes an observation which also applies to many of Welty's stories, particularly to a "A Curtain of Green": "By focusing on the natural world, then blending it with emotions of her characters through similes, [Welty] puts character and place together in dynamic relationship" (189). A dynamic relationship obviously exists between Mrs. Larkin and her garden, and the overriding characteristic of that relationship is tension.

Noting that the "rich blackness of the soil" and the "extreme fertility" of the garden "formed at once a preoccupation and a challenge to Mrs. Larkin" (108), Welty juxtaposes the abundance of the landscape against the apparent emptiness of Mrs. Larkin's family and community life. As for the other women of the town the only "place" to which Welty ever attaches them is a bedroom window: we never see them in a natural setting. The contrast between the "setting" of these women's lives and the "setting" of Mrs. Larkin's life intensifies the isolation of all of the women in the story and points to the barrenness of the lives of women in Larkin's Hill. This lack of meaningful activity, Carol Manning points out, leads to pettiness and inhumanity (54). Also contributing to the tension of the story is the fact that the rain, which usually came every afternoon by two o'clock, has not yet arrived. Even the women who only watch Mrs. Larkin and do not vigorously pursue gardening themselves are "waiting for the rain" (107).

What Welty illustrates with her description of the women's activities in "A Curtain of Green" is a pattern of ordering one's universe which MacKethan notes about Welty's fictional world in general: "Man, seeking his own identity, 'attaches' himself to a place because it offers a concrete mechanism through which he can order and hold onto the beliefs that give meaning to his life" (182). With Mrs. Larkin, however, we have a character attaching herself to a place of confusion and disorder and working energetically, obsessively, to promote even more confusion. Yet, the action itself has become the ordering device for Mrs. Larkin's universe. That the woman's frantic activities are a ritual to ease her sense of loss is clearly established early in the story. So, too, is the summer rain regarded ritualistically, as "a regular thing, [which] would come about two o'clock in the afternoon" (107). But on the day that the events of the story occur, two conditions arise which signal a disruption of the ritual: the rains have not come by late afternoon; and Mrs. Larkin has finally come to "one of the last patches of uncultivated ground" which she is clearing for some new shrubs (109). Clearly, Mrs. Larkin is approaching a point of crisis or catharsis: her gardening has provided her with a "curtain" of forgetfulness, but now she is running out of "uncultivated ground."

This subtle detail provides the operational metaphor for the story: with no new ground toward which to direct her energy, Mrs. Larkin will have to return to some area of the garden that she has already cultivated; there, she will have to nurture what already exists, or destroy the product of past efforts and begin all over again. As long as she has new ground to cultivate, she does not have to concern herself with past labors—does not have to deal with memory. She can simply move forward or in circles, drawing a curtain of green behind her. But, on the day that she reaches the last patch of uncultivated earth, "memory tightened about her easily, without any prelude or warning or even despair" (109). She sees "the fragrant chinaberry tree, suddenly tilting, dark and slow like a cloud, leaning down to her husband" (109). She recalls the absolute incredibility of not being able to control the events occurring before her eyes. When the flashback ends, Mrs. Larkin notices the stillness of her garden—the stasis of her world. The wind has ceased; birds have hushed: "The sun seemed clamped to the side of the sky. Everything had stopped once again, the stillness had mesmerized the stems of the plants, and the leaves went suddenly into thickness" (109).

To break the stillness, Mrs. Larkin calls angrily to Jamey, the black boy whom she occasionally hires to work in the garden. Suddenly, irrationally, she is infuriated by Jamey's "look of docility" (110), and what happens next is crucial to understanding the story: Mrs. Larkin moves toward Jamey with her hoe, notices that "he was lost in some impossible dream of his own" (110), and raises her hoe above his head as if to strike. Questions about life and death flash through her consciousness: "Was it not possible to compensate? To punish? To protest?" (111). The answer to her questions arrives in the form of rain, the natural occurrence which has come in its own time. Realizing that humans have no control over accidents of nature—a tree falling in the yard, the rain coming at dusk instead of at two o'clock—Mrs. Larkin lowers her hoe. Human beings, she concedes, cannot control nature, cannot even make sense sometimes of the events of their lives: but they can control their own actions. Standing close to Jamey, she "listened to the rain falling. It was so gentle. It was so full—the sound of the end of waiting" (111).

Ironically, Mrs. Larkin reaches the understanding toward which she has been ceaselessly striving by realizing that there is no rational explanation for the tragedy in her life, the separation from a husband with whom she passionately desires a reunion. "It has come, she thought senselessly, her head lifting and her eyes looking without understanding at the sky which had begun to move, to fold nearer in softening, dissolving clouds" (111). Once the grieving widow rejects the ratiocination which has paralyzed her since her husband's death, her world begins to move again. She looks forward to "the loud and gentle night of rain. . . . The day's work would be over in the garden. She would lie in bed, her arms tired at her sides and in motionless peace: against that which was inexhaustible, there was no defense" (111). Then Mrs. Larkin faints, and as she lies there among her flowers with the rain falling on woman and garden alike, Jamey looks at her "unknowing face, white and rested under its bombardment" (112); then, before running away, he calls to her until she stirs.

Critics have not dealt very thoroughly with the perplexing conclusion to "A Curtain of Green." Ruth M. Vande Kieft says the only relief from pain with which a reader leaves this story comes from "the perception of some kind of order in the work itself and of truth seen and faced, and the catharsis of pity and fear" (32). Michael Kreyling believes that the woman's unconsciousness is her passage from the modernist world of self-conscious isolation into a natural, "unseen world" where "the lost intangibles of vital human existence would once again appear as 'living realities'" (51). But since the story ends with Mrs. Larkin in a state of semi-consciousness and the last recorded impression of her stresses her "unknowing face," it seems unreasonable to conclude that she has had any revelation beyond the acceptance of her "unknowingness." Moreover, Welty reminds us that even if Mrs. Larkin learns to deal with her husband's death, she still faces a hostile, or at best, indifferent human community as represented by the other women of Larkin's Hill.

Her isolation, therefore, is neither totally self-imposed nor entirely solipsistic. The author inserts this reminder at the very end of the story by having Jamey recall that all the while Mrs. Larkin had been standing over him he had heard "the oblivious crash of the windows next door being shut when the rain started" (112). If Mrs. Larkin has succeeded in becoming "one of her own cultivations" (Kreyling 51) by merging with the natural world, then the community which promptly shuts itself away from natural phenomena will surely continue to close itself against an "over-vigorous, disreputable, and heedless" woman (107). Louis Rubin notes that human communities in Welty's fictions "are founded on the agreement . . . not to admit to the existence of chaos and violence that cannot be controlled, explained, scaled down to manageable proportion" (111). It is quite possible, then, that Mrs. Larkin's realizations will only further isolate her from human society.

By bringing our attention back to the women in the windows of Larkin's Hill, Welty demonstrates a concern for the whole female community and not just a concern for Mrs. Larkin alone. Not directly, but subliminally, Welty shows us the sad results of a patriarchal cultural bias which deprives women of meaningful work and productive outlets for creative expression. Instead, the acceptable feminine sphere in the small Southern town is the garden club meeting (not the garden) in which the members discuss "what constitutes] an appropriate vista, or an effect of restfulness, or even harmony of color" (108), or the dressing table, where women may sit and brush "studiously at their hair" (108). When Mrs. Larkin does regain consciousness, she may retain her sense of relief over accepting her husband's death as an irrational occurrence that she can never understand. Whether she can penetrate her garden wall, whether she can find meaning for her own life as a woman without a husband around which to order her existence, Welty leaves unanswered. At the end of "A Curtain of Green," Mrs. Larkin's choices as a woman in Larkin's Hill seem quite limited: to become like her neighbors, to take her seat behind a window, she will have to cease being a woman with the vitality, the passion, and penchant for prolific growth to which her garden is testimony. Welty does not push the narrative to this either/or conclusion.

Welty's quiet open-endedness in the final scene of "A Curtain of Green" contrasts starkly with Steinbeck's direct declaration of outcomes. Clearly, Mary Teller's self absorption in "The White Quail" is complete: she delivers her last spoken words of the story from behind her locked bedroom door. Her husband's final words are "Oh, Lord, I'm so lonely!" (37). Steinbeck's story lays out a dialectic discourse of cause and effect: the obsessive female gardener seeks stasis, perfection, self absorption; she takes societal expectations of idealized womanhood to a neurotic extreme. Her male counterpart commits symbolic murder out of anger and frustration. On the other hand, Welty's obsessive gardener seeks growth and change, a shattering of societal constructs, and release from self-absorption. She resists performing an act of murder to balance out the random cruelty of the universe, a randomness that has left her widowed, lonely, and frustrated.

The comparison of these two stories and their varied implementation of the "woman as garden" motif points to the influence of gender perspectives. Though neither author delivers conclusive conflict resolutions, Steinbeck more clearly than Welty blames the male's obsession with female purity for the loneliness and neurosis of humankind. The final words in "The White Quail" are spoken by the man who has co-created his own despair as he looks through his living room window at the perfect garden. Whereas Mary Teller aims to keep out the rough and tangled world, which includes a consummated marriage, Welty's Mrs. Larkin creates a rough and tangled landscape in her effort to come to terms with the destruction of her marital union. Steinbeck's exploration of the male perspective clearly accounts for major differences between the two authors' social commentary: while "A Curtain of Green" emphasizes a process of healing by focusing on human *need*, "The White Quail" focuses on *blame*.

NOTE

1. My discussion of "The White Quail" as it appears in this current essay reiterates my original reading of that story as it appeared in "Steinbeck's Cloistered Women."

WORKS CITED

Barbour, Brian. "Steinbeck as a Short Story Writer." *A Study Guide to Steinbeck's "The Long Valley."* Ed. Tetsumaro Hayashi. Ann Arbor, MI: Pierian Press, 1976.

Hadella, Charlotte. "Steinbeck's Cloistered Women." *The Steinbeck Question.* Ed. Donald R. Noble. Troy, New York: Whitson Publishing Company, 1993.

Kreyling, Michael. "Modernism in Welty's *A Curtain of Green and Other Stories.*" *Southern Quarterly* 20.4 (Summer 1982): 40–53.

MacKethan, Lucinda Hardwick. *The Dream of Arcady: Place and Time in Southern Literature.* Baton Rouge: Louisiana State UP, 1980.

Mannin, Carol S. *With Ears Opening Like Morning Glories: Eudora Welty and the Love of Story Telling.* Westport, CT: Greenword Press, 1985.

Mitchell, Marilyn. "Steinbeck's Strong Women: Feminine Identity in the Short Stories." *Steinbeck's Women: Essays in Criticism.* Ed. Tetsumaro Hayashi. Muncie, IN: Ball State University Press, 1979.

Owens, Louis. *John Steinbeck's Re-Vision of America.* Athens: University of Georgia Press, 1985.

Renner, Stanley. "Mary Teller and Sue Bridehead: Birds of a Feather in "The White Quail" and *Jude the Obscure.*" *Steinbeck Quarterly* 18 (1985).

———. "Sexual Idealism and Violence in "The White Quail." *Steinbeck Quarterly* 17 (1984).

Schmidt, Peter. *The Heart of the Story: Eudora Welty's Short Fiction.* Jackson: University of Mississippi Press, 1991.

Simpson, Arthur. "The White Quail": A Portrait of an Artist." *A Study Guide to Steinbeck's "The Long Valley."* Ed. Tetsumaro Hayashi. Ann Arbor, MI: Pierian Press, 1976.

Steinbeck, John. *The Long Valley.* New York: Viking Press, 1986. All page numbers for the parenthetical citations of Steinbeck's stories discussed here refer to this edition.

Vande Kieft, Ruth M. "Eudora Welty: The Question of Meaning." *Southern Quarterly* 20.4 (Summer 1982): 28–39.

Welty, Eudora. *The Collected Stories of Eudora Welty.* New York: Harcourt Brace Jovanovich, 1980. All page numbers for the parenthetical citations of Welty's stories discussed here refer to this edition.

Chronology

1902	John Ernst Steinbeck born on February 27, in Salinas, California, to John Ernst II and Olive Hamilton Steinbeck.
1919	Graduates from Salinas High School.
1920–25	Attends Stanford and works as laborer intermittently. Publishes first short stories in *The Stanford Spectator*.
1925	Drops out of Stanford and goes to New York. Works as construction laborer and reports for the *American* newspaper.
1926	Returns to California; writes stories and novels.
1929	His first novel, *Cup of Gold*, published.
1930	Marries Carol Henning.
1932	*The Pasture of Heaven*, a novel, published. Moves to Los Angeles.
1933	*To a God Unknown*, a novel, published. Returns to Monterey. *The Red Pony* appears in two parts in *North American Review*.
1934	Mother dies.
1935	*Tortilla Flat* is published. Father dies.
1936	*In Dubious Battle*, a novel, is published. Travels to Mexico.
1937	*Of Mice and Men* is published. Travels to Europe and later from Oklahoma to California with migrants.

1938   *Their Blood Is Strong*, nonfiction, is published. A collection of short stories, *The Long Valley*, is published.

1939   *The Grapes of Wrath* is published. Elected to the National Institute of Arts and Letters.

1940   *The Grapes of Wrath* wins the Pulitzer Prize. *The Forgotten Village*, a documentary, is produced. Goes on research trip with Edward Ricketts to the Sea of Cortez.

1941   *Sea of Cortez* published with Edward Ricketts.

1942   *The Moon Is Down* published. Divorces. Writes script *Bombs Away* for the U.S. Air Force.

1943   Moves to New York City; marries Gwendolyn Conger. In Europe, covers the war as correspondent for the *New York Herald Tribune*.

1944   Writes script for Alfred Hitchcock's *Lifeboat*. A son, Thom, is born.

1945   *Cannery Row*, a novel, is published. *The Red Pony* published in four parts.

1946   A second son, John IV, is born.

1947   *The Wayward Bus*, a novel, is published. *The Pearl*, a novella, is published. Travels in Russia with photographer Robert Capa.

1948   *A Russian Journal*, an account of his 1947 tour of Russia, is published. Divorces.

1950   *Burning Bright*, a novella, is published. Marries Elaine Anderson Scott. Writes script for *Viva Zapata!*

1951   *The Log from the Sea of Cortez*, the narrative part of *Sea of Cortez*, is published.

1952   *East of Eden* published.

1954   *Sweet Thursday*, a sequel to *Cannery Row*, published.

1957   *The Short Reign of Pippen IV*, a novel, is published.

1958   *Once There Was a War*, a collection of his wartime dispatches, is published.

1960   Takes three-month tour of America with his dog Charley.

1961	*The Winter of Our Discontent*, his twelfth and final novel, published.
1962	*Travels with Charley*, the journal of his 1960 tour, published. Awarded Nobel Prize for Literature.
1964	Awarded the United States Medal of Freedom and a Press Medal of Freedom.
1966	*American and Americans*, reflections on contemporary America, published.
1966–67	Reports from Vietnam for *Newsday*.
1968	Dies of severe heart attack in New York City on December 20.

Contributors

HAROLD BLOOM is Sterling Professor of the Humanities at Yale University. Educated at Cornell and Yale universities, he is the author of more than 30 books, including *Shelley's Mythmaking* (1959), *Blake's Apocalypse* (1963), *Yeats* (1970), *The Anxiety of Influence* (1973), *A Map of Misreading* (1975), *Kabbalah and Criticism* (1975), *Agon: Toward a Theory of Revisionism* (1982), *The American Religion* (1992), *The Western Canon* (1994), *Omens of Millennium: The Gnosis of Angels, Dreams, and Resurrection* (1996), *Shakespeare: The Invention of the Human* (1998), *How to Read and Why* (2000), *Genius: A Mosaic of One Hundred Exemplary Creative Minds* (2002), *Hamlet: Poem Unlimited* (2003), *Where Shall Wisdom Be Found?* (2004), *Jesus and Yahweh: The Names Divine* (2005), and *Till I End My Song: A Gathering of Last Poems* (2010). In addition, he is the author of hundreds of articles, reviews, and editorial introductions. In 1999, Professor Bloom received the American Academy of Arts and Letters' Gold Medal for Criticism. He has also received the International Prize of Catalonia, the Alfonso Reyes Prize of Mexico, and the Hans Christian Andersen Bicentennial Prize of Denmark.

RICHARD F. PETERSON has been a professor of English at Southern Illinois University Carbondale and is coeditor of *John Steinbeck: From Salinas to the World* and *John Steinbeck: East and West*. He also has published texts on Joyce and Yeats.

LOUIS OWENS was a professor of English and Native American Studies and director of creative writing at the University of California, Davis, at the time of his death in 2002. He was the author of The Grapes of Wrath: *Trouble in the Promised Land* and served on the advisory board of *Steinbeck*

Quarterly. He was also a novelist and published *Other Destinies: Understanding the American Indian Novel* and other works.

JOHN H. TIMMERMAN is a professor at Calvin College. His titles include *John Steinbeck's Fiction: The Aesthetics of the Road Taken.* He also has written on Frost, Eliot, and others. His work includes devotional books as well as short fiction and creative nonfiction.

ROBERT M. BENTON is retired from the English faculty at Central Washington University. He has been a consultant to the National Steinbeck Center in Salinas and has made various presentations on Steinbeck.

SUSAN SHILLINGLAW is a professor at San Jose State University. She has published many titles on Steinbeck, including *A Journey into Steinbeck's California* and Penguin editions of Steinbeck's work. She has been an editor of *Steinbeck Quarterly* and *The Steinbeck Newsletter.*

CHRISTOPHER S. BUSCH is a professor at Hillsdale College in Michigan.

JOHN DITSKY was an emeritus professor in the English department at the University of Windsor, Ontario. His work includes *Essays on "East of Eden"* and *Critical Essays on Steinbeck's "The Grapes of Wrath."* He was chairman of the editorial board of the *Steinbeck Quarterly* and senior vice president of the International John Steinbeck Society. He also published volumes of poetry.

MIMI REISEL GLADSTEIN teaches at the University of Texas at El Paso, where she also has performed numerous administrative tasks including being chairwoman of the English department. She is the author of the *Indestructible Woman in Faulkner, Hemingway, and Steinbeck.* She has won international awards for her contributions to Steinbeck studies.

STEPHEN K. GEORGE has been a professor at Brigham Young University–Idaho. He has edited or coedited various texts, including *John Steinbeck: A Centennial Tribute, John Steinbeck's Sense of Place,* and *The Moral Philosophy of John Steinbeck.* He is a cofounder of *The Steinbeck Review* and the New Steinbeck Society of America; with the help of others, he founded the John Steinbeck Society of America. He has received awards for his Steinbeck scholarship and teaching.

CHARLOTTE COOK HADELLA is a professor in the English and writing program at Southern Oregon University. Her Steinbeck scholarship includes the Twayne Masterworks Series book *Of Mice and Men: A Kinship of Powerlessness* and numerous articles on the fiction of John Steinbeck. She has been on the editorial board of the *Steinbeck Quarterly.*

Bibliography

Ariki, Kyoko, and Luchen Li and Scott Pugh, ed. *John Steinbeck's Global Dimensions.* Lanham, Md.: Scarecrow Press, 2008.

Beegel, Susan F., and Susan Shillinglaw and Wesley N. Tiffney, Jr. *Steinbeck and the Environment: Interdisciplinary Approaches.* Tuscaloosa; London: University of Alabama Press, 1997.

Coers, Donald V., and Paul D. Ruffin, and Robert J. DeMott, ed. *After* The Grapes of Wrath: *Essays on John Steinbeck in Honor of Tetsumaro Hayashi.* Athens: Ohio University Press, 1995.

Ditsky, John. *John Steinbeck and the Critics.* Rochester, N.Y.; Woodbridge, UK: Camden House, 2000.

———. "John Steinbeck, the Interior Landscape, and Tragic Depletion." *South Dakota Review* 32, no. 1 (Spring 1994): 106–15.

———. "A Kind of Play: Dramatic Elements in John Steinbeck's 'The Chrysanthemums.'" *Wascana Review of Contemporary Poetry and Short Fiction* 21, no. 1 (Spring 1986): 62–72.

———. "Steinbeck's 'Slav Girl' and the Role of the Narrator in 'The Murder.'" *Steinbeck Quarterly* 22, nos. 3–4 (Summer–Fall 1989): 68–76.

———. 'Stupid Sons of Fishes': Shared Values in John Steinbeck and the Musical Stage." *Steinbeck Studies* 15, no. 2 (Winter 2004): 107–16.

Fensch, Thomas, ed. *Conversations with John Steinbeck.* Jackson: University Press of Mississippi, 1988.

French, Warren. "John Steinbeck and American Literature." *San Jose Studies* 13, no. 2 (Spring 1987): 35–48.

———. *John Steinbeck's Fiction Revisited.* New York: Twayne Publishers; Toronto: Maxwell Macmillan Canada; New York: Maxwell Macmillan International, 1994.

Garcia, Reloy. *Steinbeck and D.H. Lawrence: Fictive Voices and the Ethical Imperative*. Muncie, Ind.: Steinbeck Society of America, English Department, Ball State University, 1972.

George, Stephen K., ed. "Global Perspectives on John Steinbeck and His Works." *Steinbeck Review* 3, no. 1 (Spring 2006): 9–164.

———. *The Moral Philosophy of John Steinbeck*. Lanham, Md.: Scarecrow Press, 2005.

Gilbert, James N. "The Influence of John Steinbeck on American Social and Criminal Justice." *Platte Valley Review* 24, no. 1 (Winter 1996): 89–99.

Girard, Maureen. "Steinbeck's 'Frightful' Story: The Conception and Evolution of 'The Snake.'" *San Jose Studies* 8, no. 2 (Spring 1982): 33–40.

Gladstein, Mimi Reisel. *The Indestructible Woman in Faulkner, Hemingway, and Steinbeck*. Ann Arbor: University Microfilms International Research Press, 1986.

———. "Steinbeck's Dysfunctional Families: A Coast-to-Coast Dilemma." *Steinbeck Review* 3, no. 1 (Spring 2006): 35–52.

Hayashi, Tetsumaro, ed. *A New Study Guide to Steinbeck's Major Works, with Critical Explications*. Metuchen, N.J.: Scarecrow Press, 1993.

———. *Steinbeck's Literary Dimension: A Guide to Comparative Studies*. Series II. Metuchen, N.J.: Scarecrow Press, 1991.

Hayashi, Tetsumaro, and Thomas J. Moore, ed. *Steinbeck's Posthumous Work: Essays in Criticism*. Muncie, Ind., U.S.A.: Steinbeck Research Institute, Department of English, College of Sciences and Humanities, Ball State University, 1989.

———. *Steinbeck's "The Red Pony": Essays in Criticism*. Muncie, Ind., U.S.A.: Steinbeck Research Institute, Department of English, Ball State University, 1988.

Hearle, Kevin. "The Pastures of Contested Pastoral Discourse." *Steinbeck Quarterly* 26, nos. 1–2 (Winter–Spring 1993): 38–45.

Higdon, David Leon. "Dionysian Madness in Steinbeck's 'The Chrysanthemums.'" *Classical and Modern Literature: A Quarterly* 11, no. 1 (Fall 1990): 59–65.

Hughes, Robert S., Jr. *John Steinbeck: A Study of the Short Fiction*. Boston: Twayne, 1989.

———. "What Went Wrong? How a 'Vintage' Steinbeck Short Story Became the Flawed *Winter of Our Discontent*." *Steinbeck Quarterly* 26, nos. 1–2 (Winter–Spring 1993): 7–12.

Johnson, Claudia Durst. *Understanding* Of Mice and Men, The Red Pony, *and* The Pearl: *A Student Casebook to Issues, Sources, and Historical Documents*. Westport, Conn.: Greenwood Press, 1997.

Lewis, Cliff, and Carroll Britch, ed. *Rediscovering Steinbeck: Revisionist Views of His Art, Politics, and Intellect*. Lewiston [N.Y.]: Edwin Mellen Press, 1989.

McCarthy, Paul. *John Steinbeck*. New York: Ungar, 1980.

McElrath, Jr., Joseph R., and Jesse S. Crisler, and Susan Shillinglaw, ed. *John Steinbeck: The Contemporary Reviews*. Cambridge; New York: Cambridge University Press, 1996.

Meyer, Michael J. *The Hayashi Steinbeck Bibliography, 1982–1996*. Lanham, Md.: Scarecrow Press, 1998.

Miller, Arthur. "John Steinbeck: Flights and Flights." *PEN America: A Journal for Writers and Readers* 4, no. 2 (2002): 17–37.

Millichap, Joseph R. *Steinbeck and Film*. New York: Ungar, 1983.

Mitchell, Marilyn L. "Steinbeck's Strong Women: Feminine Identity in the Short Stories." *Southwest Review* 61 (1976): 304–15.

Osborne, William R. "The Texts of Steinbeck's 'The Chrysanthemums.'" *Modern Fiction Studies* 12 (1966): 479–84.

Pellow, C. Kenneth. "'The Chrysanthemums' Revisited." *Steinbeck Quarterly* 22, nos. 1–2 (Winter–Spring 1989): 8–16.

Petite, Joseph. "The Invisible Woman in Steinbeck's 'The Chrysanthemums.'" *Journal of Evolutionary Psychology* 16, nos. 3–4 (August 1995): 285–91.

Plath, James. "Deflowered: Walking Students through a Harsher Reading of John Steinbeck's 'The Chrysanthemums.'" *Eureka Studies in Teaching Short Fiction* 2, no. 1 (Fall 2001): 61–75.

Railsback, Brian. *Parallel Expeditions: Charles Darwin and the Art of John Steinbeck*. Moscow, Idaho: University of Idaho Press, 1995.

Renner, Stanley. "Mary Teller and Sue Bridehead: Birds of a Feather in 'The White Quail' and *Jude the Obscure*." *Steinbeck Quarterly* 18, nos. 1–2 (Summer–Fall 1985): 35–45.

———. "The Real Woman inside the Fence in 'The Chrysanthemums.'" *MFS: Modern Fiction Studies* 31, no. 2 (Summer 1985): 305–17.

———. "Sexual Idealism and Violence in 'The White Quail.'" *Steinbeck Quarterly* 17, nos. 3–4 (1984): 76–87.

Schultz, Jeffrey, and Luchen Li. *Critical Companion to John Steinbeck: A Literary Reference to His Life and Work*. New York: Facts On File/Checkmark Books, 2005.

Shillinglaw, Susan, and Kevin Hearle, ed. *Beyond Boundaries: Rereading John Steinbeck*. Tuscaloosa, Ala.; London: University of Alabama Press, 2002.

Simmonds, Roy. *John Steinbeck: The War Years, 1939–1945*. Lewisburg, [Pa.]: Bucknell University Press; London; Cranbury, N.J.: Associated University Presses, 1996.

Timmerman, John H. *John Steinbeck's Fiction: The Aesthetics of the Road Taken*. Norman: University of Oklahoma Press, 1986.

Ware, Elaine. "Struggle for Survival: Parallel Theme and Techniques in Steinbeck's 'Flight' and Norris's *McTeague*." *Steinbeck Quarterly* 21, nos. 3–4 (Summer–Fall 1988): 96–103.

Work, James C. "Coordinate Forces in 'The Leader of the People.'" *Western American Literature* 16, no. 4 (February 1982): 279–89.

Acknowledgments

Richard F. Peterson, "Steinbeck and D. H. Lawrence." From *Steinbeck's Literary Dimension: A Guide to Comparative Studies*, edited by Tetsumaro Hayashi. Published by The Scarecrow Press. Copyright © 1972 by Tetsumaro Hayashi.

Louis Owens, "*The Red Pony*: Commitment and Quest." From *John Steinbeck's Re-Vision of America*. Copyright © 1985 by the University of Georgia Press.

John H. Timmerman, "*The Red Pony*: 'The Desolation of Loss.'" From *The Dramatic Landscape of Steinbeck's Short Stories*. Copyright © 1990 by the University of Oklahoma Press.

Robert M. Benton, "A Search for Meaning in 'Flight.'" From *Steinbeck's Short Stories in* The Long Valley: *Essays in Criticism*, edited by Tetsumaro Hayashi. Published by Ball State University. Copyright © 1991 by Tetsumaro Hayashi.

Susan Shillinglaw, "'The Chrysanthemums': Steinbeck's Pygmalion." From *Steinbeck's Short Stories in* The Long Valley: *Essays in Criticism*, edited by Tetsumaro Hayashi. Published by Ball State University. Copyright © 1991 by Tetsumaro Hayashi.

Christopher S. Busch, "Longing for the Lost Frontier: Steinbeck's Vision of Cultural Decline in 'The White Quail' and 'The Chrysanthemums.'" From *Steinbeck Quarterly* 26, nos. 3 and 4 (Summer–Fall 1993): 81–90. Copyright © 1993 by *Steinbeck Quarterly*.

John Ditsky, "'Your Own Mind Coming Out in the Garden': Steinbeck's Elusive Woman." From *John Steinbeck: the Years of Greatness, 1936–1939*, edited by Tetsumaro Hayashi. Copyright © 1993 by the University of Alabama Press.

Mimi Reisel Gladstein, "Faulkner and Steinbeck: Thematic and Stylistic Resonance in the Early Stories." From *John Steinbeck and His Contemporaries*, edited by Stephen K. George and Barbara A. Heavilin. Published by The Scarecrow Press. Copyright © 2007 by Stephen K. George and Barbara A. Heavilin.

Stephen K. George, "'Surrendering to the Feminine': Implied Author Compassion in 'The Chrysanthemums' and 'Hills Like White Elephants.'" From *John Steinbeck and His Contemporaries*, edited by Stephen K. George and Barbara A. Heavilin. Published by The Scarecrow Press. Copyright © 2007 by Stephen K. George and Barbara A. Heavilin.

Charlotte Cook Hadella, "Lonely Ladies and Landscapes: A Comparison of John Steinbeck's 'The White Quail' and Eudora Welty's 'A Curtain of Green'" From *A John Steinbeck Reader: Essays in Honor of Stephen K. George*, edited by Barbara A. Heavilin. Published by The Scarecrow Press. Copyright © 2009 by Barbara A. Heavilin.

Every effort has been made to contact the owners of copyrighted material and secure copyright permission. Articles appearing in this volume generally appear much as they did in their original publication with few or no editorial changes. In some cases, foreign language text has been removed from the original essay. Those interested in locating the original source will find the information cited above.

Index

Characters in literary works are indexed by first name (if any), followed by the name of the work in parentheses.